MA
CONTACT

MAKING CONTACT

ROB MARSHALL

BIBLE SOCIETY

British and Foreign Bible Society
Stonehill Green, Westlea, SWINDON SN5 7DG, England

First published 1993

Unless otherwise stated, quotations from the Bible are from the Good News Bible, published by the Bible Societies/HarperCollins © American Bible Society, New York, 1966, 1971 and 4th edition 1976.

A catalogue record for this book is available from the British Library

ISBN 0564 08445X

Printed in Great Britain by Biddles Ltd, Guildford
Cover design by Jane Taylor
Internal illustrations by Ian Parratt

CONTENTS

FOREWORD

Most of us see the world through the eyes of media: images from television and video dominate the majority of living rooms, newspapers carry detailed reports, and the "walkman" has replaced the book on bus and train journeys. The rapid changes in communication technology through the mass media and in our homes have vastly transformed the nature of our society and its values.

It is in this fast-moving and ever-changing world that the Church is called upon to bear witness to the Good News of the living Christ. Our need for a well-equipped, well-informed Church, which can use the resources of the media to share the Gospel could not be greater. And I believe that this simple, yet important, book is a significant contribution to the growth and mission of the local church in this vital area.

Rob Marshall encourages us to take seriously the context in which we find ourselves, and gives us plenty of good, practical advice about the ways in which Christians can make a worthwhile and potentially transforming contribution to the media in a very secular society. He shares the fruits of his wide and varied experience with his usual flair, skill, humour and effectiveness.

Rob Marshall served me as Press Secretary in the Diocese of Bradford between 1985 and 1991, where he was also a vicar in the Yorkshire Dales, Diocesan Communications Officer, and a well-known sports commentator on local radio and television! He is now Diocesan Communications Officer in the very different context of London, just over the river from me here in Southwark.

Life is never dull when Rob is around, and I hope that those who read and use this book will be infected by his obvious enthusiasm for communicating the Good News of the Gospel.

The Bishop of Southwark,
the Rt Revd Roy Williamson

ACKNOWLEDGEMENTS

I have been convinced for as long as I can remember that the churches have a unique message to share with the world, and that they need to work hard at harnessing their resources to effectively communicate the Good News of Christ to a world that seems to be so often fractured by hopelessness and fear.

I had been the Bradford Diocesan Press and Communications Officer and Priest-in-Charge of Embsay with Eastby for nearly three years when the Bible Society suggested that I should write this practical resource book for local churches who are seeking to enhance their own growth and mission by improving their internal and external communication.

Many people have supported me during the writing of this book: Bishop Roy Williamson encouraged me to take time to write it while he was Bishop of Bradford, and, after his move to Southwark, was generous in providing the Foreword; Bishop David Hope has given me the opportunity to pursue my communication interest in the challenging context of the capital city, and I am grateful to him for his friendship and support. The people of Embsay and Eastby in the Diocese of Bradford were tremendous in putting up with their "communications" vicar, and I am also grateful to Sheila Meyer who helped me draft and type the original scripts. I would also like to thank Simon Reynolds of the Bible Society for inviting me to write the book in the first place, and to Louise Kirby for her care in preparing the typescript and proofs. Many journalists and broadcasters – too many to name – have been a great source of stimulation in my work, and have convinced me that good relations between the churches and the media are crucial and need much work and effort.

Finally, and most importantly, my thanks go to my wife, Lesley, and my children, Stephen and Louisa, who have heard the stories in this book many times before, and who continue to support me in every aspect of my ministry.

Rob Marshall
London,
Ascension Day 1993

TELL ME THE OLD, OLD STORY

However contemporary we may try to be, our authority rests on an old, old story. And all this amidst a generation for whom the sense of the past is very faint. (M Ramsey, *The Christian Priest Today*, SPCK, 1972, p. 27)

THE CHURCH'S TASK

The chief task of the Christian Church is to communicate the good news that Jesus proclaimed. Few of us are likely to argue about that, yet it has been my experience that the Church has struggled — and is still struggling at all levels — to celebrate and share this good news in a fast-moving and highly technological world. Of course, we must continue to tell the story of Christ's good news with faithfulness and integrity, but, at the same time, we need to make it come alive for people in ways that engage their interest and commitment.

We are challenged to communicate with the world, to share the message of salvation and hope that is offered to us by the living Christ, and to do it in a way that changes people's hearts and lives. So how do we go about it?

Every generation is called upon to analyse the context in which it is placed and in which the gospel will be proclaimed. Some communities of Christians have found communicating the gospel a relatively easy task, but others have had to endure persecution, great hardships, and almost insurmountable hurdles. Yet it is interesting to discover that, even in the most unpromising situations and when the odds are stacked against us, opportunities still exist for direct ways of demonstrating our faith to others. In this respect, we have much to learn from our Christian forebears. Henry Chadwick (in *The Early Church*, Penguin, 1967) stresses the commitment of the early Church to spreading the message in the face of real persecution:

It is an illusion to think that persecution drove the church down to the catacombs and that the sacraments had to be celebrated in a kind of troglodyte life. Persecution, so far

from driving the church underground had the opposite effect.
When one governor in Asia Minor in the second century
began persecuting the Christians, the entire Christian popu-
lation of the region paraded before his house as a manifesto
of their faith and as a protest against the injustice. (p. 55)

Situations similar to this have been seen in the twentieth century
(which has seen more people put to death for their faith than any
previous one), a time when Christian faith has been spread by
word of mouth and at meetings, and when people have continued
to be baptized. Shortly before communism collapsed in the Soviet
Union, for example, the Bible Society sent 10,000 Bibles to be dis-
tributed in 1987. No matter what the barriers are, the message can
still get through. Communication channels are rarely closed down
completely.

Communication then is at the heart of the gospel, and the need
to communicate the message of Jesus is a crucial aspect of the
Church's life and witness. Getting the message across, making
direct, personal contact with people of all ages and backgrounds, is
to follow the example of Jesus himself. It is my intention in this
book to spell out some of the basic aspects of Christian communication which take into account the context in which we find ourselves today in the local church. However, I don't want to concentrate purely on the external concerns of Christian communication
— our concerns are internal as well. Have you noticed the link
between the two words *communi*cation and *communi*on: the com-
ing together of the gathered Church to celebrate and share in God's
presence in word and sacrament.

Communication is not simply another word for evangelism. For
although we all acknowledge that the Church is in the business of
sharing the good news of Christ with the outside world, it is
equally important to realize that a well-informed and aware
Church depends upon effective internal communication as well.

Before we examine the particular communication task and context facing today's Church, we need to start with the Christian
community's basic tool: the Bible. It provides us with the basis for
our message as well as some superb examples of the way in which
God communicates with men and women, how they communicate
with one another, and how that communication can so easily break
down.

BIBLICAL POINTERS

The Bible reveals a variety of different communication methods and models. Eddie Gibbs (in *The God Who Communicates,* Hodder & Stoughton, 1985, p. 13) suggests that God is a communicator whose methods involve words, signs, and symbols: "The Bible not only tells us what God desires to communicate, it also demonstrates that he uses a wide variety of methods to get that message across. He is a multi-media communicator."

The sheer drama of many of the Old Testament stories has been brought home to us in epic films like *Moses the Lawgiver,* however, behind the spills and thrills of the big screen are the many and varied ways in which God called individuals and communities, and the ways in which his will and purpose was made known through prophets and kings as well as through widows and orphans. The method of communication was always grounded in the reality of people's lives and the world in which they lived.

In a useful introduction to the Old Testament, J N Schofield (in *Introducing Old Testament Theology,* SCM, 1964) highlights the importance of viewing the Hebrew books as God speaking directly to his people:

> *The Old Testament writers and editors believed themselves to be part of the people whom God had chosen and called to be the medium through which he could reveal himself, and they so shaped and arranged ancient myths, national legends, traditions and history as to make them a record wherein men could find and meet God and hear speaking the revealing word.* (p. 10)

Thus in the books of the Old Testament God speaks to his people and through them he speaks to us. Schofield adds:

> *The Bible is a record of the living experiences of a living people in contact with a living God. He revealed his will by word and deed in an historical situation, and when, later, the record was written the revelation was released from a particular time and became a timeless message to successive generations.* (p. 11)

In Jesus, we discover a crucial turning point in God's way of communicating with the world. His Word, which had previously been made known through faithful and obedient people, now came into the world as flesh and blood. People were greeted with the good news and could see for themselves that the Kingdom of God had come in the form of Jesus of Nazareth. Look at the ways in which some of the writers of the New Testament expressed this:

- John 1.1–18;
- Hebrews 1.1–4;
- 1 John 1.1–4.

The success of Jesus as a communicator has been examined. He was born into a Jewish family, and would have heard the Scriptures read in the synagogue and in the temple. He would have been very aware of the great themes of the Pentateuch, the Wisdom literature, and the Prophets. Michael Green suggests:

> *He seems to have been equally at home preaching in a syna-*
> *gogue or speaking in the open air; debating with religious*
> *leaders to talking about the things of God with simple vil-*
> *lagers. He could catch and hold the attention of a large (and*
> *sometimes hungry) crowd, or give intimate instruction to a*
> *little band of committed disciples. (The Teaching of Jesus,*
> Hodder & Stoughton, 1983, p. 10)

In his teaching, Jesus used simple words and images and gave them a new meaning.

His mainly extempore teaching arose from personal conversations with individuals, small groups and large crowds. His calm, confident and reassuring delivery made everyone who thought they knew better feel extremely uncomfortable. He used images and words from the Scriptures, nature, village life, and human experience. After the ascension of Jesus, the Holy Spirit guided the apostles to continue to proclaim the words and works of Jesus. The early Christian communities, which were established as a response to the teaching of the apostles, grew because the message they proclaimed was tuned into the Holy Spirit. In this way people of different backgrounds, languages, and cultures were brought near to the Kingdom of God. The early Church was essentially a community of storytellers who preached the message of Jesus with conviction. Once again, the context of the communication was extremely important. Their message was received because it spoke with direct simplicity and integrity to the experience of those who heard it. The Bible teaches us a great deal about how God has communicated with us in the past and contains clues as to how we might proceed in our communication's task today.

MEDIA AWARENESS

To understand the context in which Christians have to work, as
they seek to "make contact" with the secular world today, we
should begin by looking at the media.

Communication has developed and improved at an alarming
rate in Western, capitalist societies over the past twenty years.
Here are some of the reasons why:

- Transport is more rapid and effective.
- The world has seemingly "shrunk" in size as a result of more
  accessible travel.
- In the UK alone, there are 220,000 miles of surfaced roads, and
  during the last 10 years, there has been a 25 per cent increase in
  the number of motorway miles.
- Nearly every household has access to a telephone.
- Fax machines are an essential tool in the business world.
- Cable and satellite technology is an increasing feature of both
  domestic and business life.

In short, we can get to places more quickly and easily; we have
more immediate access to information; and pictures, words, and
symbols — whether on radio and television or in magazines and
newspapers — are being placed before us every minute of every
day.

As Wesley Carr writes:

> *Even though the major media vary in their impact on people,
> this does not mean that we cannot describe our society as
> media saturated. It is more easy to avoid reading a news-
> paper than to turn off the television. Television is notably
> more intrusive than radio — at least to those brought up
> before its widespread availability. But in spite of such quali-
> fications, "media saturated" describes the society which we
> know and of which we are members. Wherever we turn there
> is no avoiding the direct or dispersed impact of the mass
> media. (Ministry and the Media, SPCK, 1991, p. 58)*

All this reminds us of a fact of life that the churches can so easily
ignore: people are saturated by the media. In magazines, newspapers, radio, and television a whole variety of stories, images,
opinions, morals, and agendas are presented to us, and much of
what we think about places, people, and issues are completely
dominated by the media.

You only have to think of the media coverage during a general election campaign. Many newspapers take a particular political stance and the "pure news" is crudely filtered through an editorial process that many readers are not aware of. However, this does not only happen at election times. Radio and television producers, normally more unbiased politically than their newspaper colleagues, are nevertheless looking for that soundbite (a clip of audio tape that can be used on a news bulletin) or picture that will improve their coverage. Obviously, such selectivity can distort a piece of news.

The competition for news and good stories is cut-throat in our media-dominated society. Despite this, at all levels within the churches there seems to have been only a very slow realization of the media's power and impact on people, an influence that starts at a very early age. This has clear implications not only for people who enter the Church from the world outside; it also means that the Church's internal communications are seen in a completely different light because of people's experience and expectations in the world outside. Media awareness is a conscious consideration of the effect that the media have on all aspects of our lives. Children, education, marriage, money, sex, morals, family life, old age, death, priorities, people, and places are all affected by the media. And so are we. The extent to which we are affected and what we should do about it is part of our Christian discipleship.

WHAT IS OUR CHURCH SAYING?

So far, we have established that the chief task of the Church is to communicate the gospel in a context where communication is the name of the game. The Bible provides us with the message we are to share with others, as well as many examples of how to go about this; and Christian tradition has wrestled with the difficulties of proclaiming the message in many difficult and different circumstances. Today, it is vital that we look around and understand the context in which we are working, and the people to whom we are proclaiming the message, if we are to communicate the gospel effectively.

We must all begin in our own church. If you take just a few minutes to think about it, you will realize that some of the basic things that we take for granted actually say things to people who visit our church for the first time:

THIS MORNING CHILDREN, THE VICAR HAS COME TO DEMONSTRATE
THE DIFFERENCE BETWEEN TRANSUBSTANTIATION
AND CONSUBSTANTIATION.

- Does the building look attractive from the outside? Is it well-painted, litter-free and does it look loved?

- Are the notice-boards clear and effective? What are they saying to people about what goes on inside?

- Is the entrance to our church welcoming? Do people feel that they are entering a place where they will soon feel at home?

- Does the lighting in our church produce the right effect? How can it be improved?

- Can people actually hear what is being said in the church? If there is a public-address system, is it a good one or does it intrude?

- Is there literature at the back of the church that introduces the building and what goes on among the worshipping members of the church? Is it well displayed or a complete mess? Is it frequently checked so that it is up to date?

- When people arrive, do we say hello to them?

- Are people who are taking part in the service well turned out and looking pleased to be leading God's worship? Are people competent at reading lessons and prayers, and giving talks?

- Is the music of an acceptable quality? Do people know when to sing. Has the music been well prepared and chosen?

Some may respond negatively to such preliminary questions and say that the Church should not be primarily concerned with issues such as these. However, we have to put ourselves where people are, just as Jesus did. People's expectations are much greater now, and professional standards of presentation on television and radio are obviously improving all the time. Even cathedral choirs are producing compact discs of their singing. How something looks and sounds is counted as important. Of course, people are not expecting a *Songs of Praise* or a cathedral service in every chapel and church in the land, but we do have a responsibility to make our churches as user-friendly and welcoming as possible.

DO WE SPEAK TO ONE ANOTHER?

After considering how we appear to those who come across us in our churches for the first time, it is important that we also pay close attention to all aspects of internal communication within our churches. Each church will have its own structure. Anglican churches have a Parochial Church Council (PCC), which governs the finances of the church, along with two elected churchwardens and the incumbent (or vicar). Roman Catholic churches have Parish Councils which advise and make an input into local policy, with the final responsibility resting with the parish priest. In some of the Free Churches, there are trustees or elders who are elected by the congregation to oversee the life of the church in conjunction with the minister. Whatever way your church is organized, make sure people know about it and how it works. Look at ways in which the structure can regularly be "oiled" so that information can flow more freely.

Let us begin outside the church. Usually the denominational headquarters (diocesan office, district office, regional offices) will be filtering information and items of interest to the parishes. Because of their very busy lives, it is often difficult for church leaders to disseminate all the necessary information from the wider Church to the members of his/her own church.

In the diocese of London, I am currently responsible for a bulletin which goes out to all stipendiary clergy in the diocese on a monthly basis. On average, more than forty items come from various groups and societies who want to keep the clergy informed about courses, lectures, events, and projects that will genuinely be of interest to many in the wider Church. And yet it is very difficult to assess how effectively that information is then shared with local church members.

Another problem area in the sharing of information throughout the church family is the various fellowships and groups that make up the life of the church (prayer, Bible study, choir, mothers' unions, men's supper club, etc.). Do they all know what the other groups are doing? There can be immense isolationism in our churches. Later, we shall look at the importance of a weekly noticesheet and/or the parish magazine. An earlier need here, though, is surely a church diary in which key events can be kept so that dates do not clash and everyone knows what is going on.

Church members and leaders need to work hard at internal communication. It is so easy for communication barriers and hurdles to emerge which are then difficult to break down again. One of the key areas is often finance. Do people know how much it costs to run the church? Do they know the amount given to the church last week? Do they understand the covenanting system? Such basic issues are often not communicated and therefore not addressed. One problem is that information dispersal costs money which is a reason why notice-boards are not changed, posters not printed, and painting not done.

THROUGH COMMUNITY AND PRESS

Once a church feels that it has internal coherence and that people know what is happening, it is surprising how much more effective a congregation can be in communicating its work to the local community.

This happens in a variety of ways:

*   By word of mouth — "something is going on in that church".
*   Events are being organized that people get to hear about.
*   The local press become aware of a community that has something to say and its corporate life reflects this.
*   The parish magazine is widely read and looks interesting.
*   Relationships with local schools, health centres, and community groups improve and the church becomes a part of the local network.
*   Baptisms, weddings, and funerals are regarded as ways of building up communications with those who come to the church at times of need or for significant events.

If evangelism is to be taken seriously, a Christian community must realize that it has a twofold dimension to its life and witness. The first is internal — making sure that each member of the Body of Christ is helping and assisting other members to create a real sense of love and community. The second, a much more ignored dimension, is the need to proclaim the message of Jesus to those who live in the community around us so that our church can grow and flourish.

Our communication should be both internal and external. It also needs to be proactive as well as reactive. Particularly in view of the demands made by the media, there is a tendency for the Churches at national level to be always reacting to events and happenings. We are slowly learning that that this is no longer an honourable way forward for the gospel. (We deal with much of the reactive/proactive argument in the rest of the book.)

WHAT IS THE SUBSTANCE?

Before we make a closer examination of some of the tasks facing the Church in a media-dominated world, I would like to offer you a simple response to a basic question that is facing us. What, ultimately, are we trying to say to people? Who are we trying to communicate with? What is the Christian message we must try to get across internally and externally?

In the lecture given in 1991 in Leeds, entitled "Theology of Communication", Dr D E Jenkins described the Trinity as "An excellent way of pointing to how God has communicated, and still comunicates, with us. He is God the Father over all and beyond; God the Son, down to earth and one of us; God the Holy Spirit, living within us and working between us". Bishop Jenkins is affirming the many different ways in which we experience God, and the many different ways in which God reveals himself to us. Our task, as Christians, is to discern the ways in which God is made known to us and experienced by us, and to communicate that variety and distinctiveness to the many and varied situations that exist in the world today.

In most Christian traditions, we end our worship and are sent out into the world with words that invoke the name of the Trinity, whether it is a blessing or the Grace:

• The Grace of our Lord Jesus Christ, and the love of God, and the fellowship of the Holy Spirit be with us all, ever more. Amen.

or

• The blessing of God Almighty, the Father, the Son, and the Holy Spirit, rest upon you and remain with you always. Amen.

These are words to sustain and support us, of course, but they can also serve as a challenge to us, calling on us to be discerning and distinctive as we communicate with the world outside, and to be sensitive and effective as we communicate with each other inside the Church.

Being open to God is the most important aspect of any Christian act of communication. David Winter emphasizes the importance of discerning God's presence in a world full of distractions: "God communicates with us. That, for me, is the single most important thing one can know about the world we live in." (*Truth in the Son,* Hodder & Stoughton, 1985, p. 16.)

Thus the thrust of the message we are called to communicate is that God is truly Father, Son, and Holy Spirit. This is the message that those within and those outside the Church need to hear. Through the spoken, written, and visual word it is clear that more can be done to improve communication in the Church today. In this book we look at various practical ways of improving communication in the local church, bearing in mind the increasing demands of the media. This involves a basic understanding of the need to be proactive. It is not enough to be simply *reacting* to events, deadlines and issues; *proactive* strategy demands a simple yet effective attempt to communicate afresh the words and works of Jesus. We begin by going back to the most primitive form of interpersonal communication: talking to other people in speeches and sermons with God very much in mind.

THE POWER OF SPEECH

The Minister, as educator or preacher presents the gospel as a way of discipleship, which is to be studied, learned and lived. (W. Carr, *Ministry and the Media*, SPCK, 1991, p. 117.)

PREACHING AND PUBLIC SPEAKING

The proclamation of the Word of God through preaching and public speaking remains a very important feature of church life today. The media explosion of the past few decades, which acts as a backdrop to the delivery of sermons and talks, has obviously affected the way in which people listen, respond, and absorb the message. Cynics might well say that empty pews and seats in many chapels and churches are a result of boredom and a sense of predictability concerning the message that is being communicated. Others might say that a drop in church attendance is the result of many factors, of which a failure to find the right words and pictures is just one.

Increasing attention will have to be given to interpersonal communication if the churches are to communicate effectively in the future. In seminars that I have conducted, I find many people saying that they are bored during sermons. "A vicar standing in a pulpit, 20 feet above contradiction, is not my idea of enjoying a Sunday morning" is a commonly held view.

The challenge is to see how we can use sermons and talks more effectively to enhance the Church's proclamation of the gospel. Interpersonal communication began in the Old Testament, between God and various individuals, and remains crucial in the Christian Church today.

BIBLICAL BACKGROUND

Some of the great dramas of the Old Testament occur when God converses or intervenes directly with his people. His famous conversations with Abraham, Moses, and the Prophets (cf. Genesis 22.1–22; Exodus 6.2–8; Isaiah 52.7–10) are good examples. Frank Jefkins (in *Public Relations Techniques*, Butterworth Heinemann,

1988) has traced the history of public relations back to the Bible and suggests that it begins in the Old Testament:

Where does the history of PR begin? Probably as soon as people found it necessary to communicate in order to make themselves understood. It exists whether we like it or not. It would not be improper to suggest that the Bible is full of examples, with tablets of stone and scrolls of papyrus as early media. (p. 5)

The incarnation was in itself God's greatest act of communication; and, as you read through the Gospels, it is almost impossible to disagree with the view that Jesus was a brilliant communicator. He was a preacher and speaker par excellence: he spoke eloquently using words that people understood; his sentences were simple yet profound; he had exactly the right balance between religious imagery and everyday experience. He says in John 16.25: "I have used figures of speech, but will speak to you plainly about the Father."

A close analysis of Jesus' ministry will reveal that he always found the correct approach and the right words. Study closely the Sermon on the Mount (Matthew 5) and you will see a master communicator at work. In St Mark's Gospel, as the pressure from the religious authorities and critics began to increase, Jesus found words and phrases that enabled him to carry on. There is much that we can learn from the ministry of Jesus as we seek to make his message known today.

Jesus' influence continued in the Book of Acts and the Epistles. The early Church did not meet at 9.30 a.m. for morning worship in a pleasant church, with hymnbooks, a noticesheet, a microphone, and a pulpit. The proclamation of Jesus' resurrection was done informally as people gathered together, but it was done with great relevance and conviction.

NOT JUST THE CLERGY

The increasing involvement of the laity in the wider life of the Church in recent years has seen a steady rise in the number of lay-people preaching and giving talks. More and more laypeople are taking an active roll in theological debate, decision-making, and in the day-to-day running of churches; this means that more people are joining in the debate about how the Church should proceed in its ministry and mission.

It is therefore vital that we have an effective and confident laity. Some are called by God to preach and expound the Word in the form of public worship. Others may have gifts in the field of stewardship, finance, education, healing, or another area of the Church's life, and will want to contribute in the form of giving talks and sharing their gifts with others more informally.

Making contact with others inside and outside the Church, interpersonal communication, is therefore the task of both clergy and laity and this will be true for all the other communication activities referred to in this book.

PREACHING

It is vital that we make a clear distinction between preaching and public speaking, even though both demand the same degree of commitment and professionalism. The basic proclamation, that Christ has been raised from the dead, was the message preached by the first Christians. Throughout the centuries, denominations and traditions have varied in the emphasis placed on the importance of preaching in contrast to the celebration of the sacraments in which the risen Christ is also encountered.

In Canon B 18 of the Church of England, for example, we read the following:

> *In every parish church a sermon shall be preached at least once each Sunday except for some reasonable cause approved by the bishop of the Diocese. The preacher shall endeavour himself with care and sincerity to minister the word of truth, to the glory of God and the edification of the people.*

Good preaching springs out of a life of faith. Some of the greatest preachers have been poor communicators in the modern sense of the word. It is true that a good preacher will normally be someone who can give a clear, concise, and intelligible exposition of the Christian faith. The media-saturated environment in which we now find ourselves demands that our preaching and sermons are "plugged into" the world.

Most preachers are aware of the kind of problems they are likely to experience when preaching to a congregation containing few regular churchgoers. Many people today are ignorant about

Christianity and the Church. This ignorance can lead to boredom and misunderstanding. There is also a certain indifference among many when it comes to a sermon: what has that to do with me? There is the basic problem of unbelief; some 94 per cent of the population no longer go to church on a Sunday.

Yet for many ministers the sermon is the highlight of the week. It is the opportunity to climb into the pulpit and expound the Word of God to the faithful and, hopefully, to reach at least some who are seeking a deeper understanding of what the good news is all about.

Sermons should reflect life as people experience it and not be idealistic. It is important to reflect on where people are, rather than where we think they are. Positive feedback from congregations inevitably comes in sermons that make reference to people and places that they know. In Lent 1992 I preached a sermon on temptation at All Saints, Margaret Street. For some unknown reason I mentioned the name of the village of Giggleswick in the Yorkshire Dales. A few people actually referred to the central theme of the sermon in the church courtyard after the service, but more than a dozen told me that they had been to Giggleswick. The point of the sermon had not been lost but what I had said had been reinforced by a place name that meant a great deal to some people. Similarly, it is wise to refer to current national or international events, or a television or radio programme or sporting event that has captured the country's attention. Thus you need to take people's minds and hearts into a world with which they can clearly identify.

GIVING TALKS

When I was a curate at Kirkstall in Leeds, the following was a typical week. Preaching at Evensong on the Sunday was followed by a talk to the mothers' union on the Monday, a school assembly on Wednesday, another at the High School the following day, and a men's fellowship meeting that evening. There were usually a couple of funeral addresses as well. Most clergy find their week littered with occasions when they are expected to talk (not preach) to other people. As I mentioned above, this is also the case for an increasing number of laity who give up their time to share their faith or skills with others. Many Christian bodies (mothers' union, uniformed organizations, Christian Aid) rely on people moving around various church groups and organizations to get the message across via talks.

During my time as a communications officer, I have spoken to Rotary Clubs, Inner Wheels, chambers of commerce, school prize givings, sports dinners and journalistic gatherings, mothers' unions, youth clubs, young wives' groups and clergy chapters. They all have their own particular nuances and demands. It does not matter whether there are ten women huddled around a fire in an otherwise freezing church hall or 300 at a well-organized conference: the communication challenge is the same.

The most obvious tasks to face any church member giving a talk can be listed as follows:

* An afternoon or evening talk to a group of up to 30 people in a small room. The format usually consists of club business, introduction by the chairperson/president, the talk, and questions.
* Informal talk to a group of children/adults in a much larger building where notes are inappropriate and you are asked to say a few words of introduction.
* The after-dinner speech where people have consumed food and drink and are usually sitting at tables. The talk nearly always comes at the end of the meal and after a series of other short addresses.

We now move on to more practical advice about standing up and preaching or talking in a group of people. We have to proceed on the understanding that we want to communicate a certain message and then establish the best way of doing this.

STEPS IN THE RIGHT DIRECTION

What kind of talk?

Always establish at the outset what kind of a talk you have been asked to give. If you are preaching, it should be obvious! Are you preaching on a special Sunday in the Church's year and/or on a special Sunday in the life of the church to which you are visiting? It may indeed be both. On Palm Sunday of 1992 I was asked to preach at St Augustine's, Kilburn, on the occasion of the climax of the parish stewardship campaign. There was more than one theme obvious there! Is your address part of a series of sermons and addresses? Will you be preaching from the pulpit? Will there be any children in the congregation? It is important to glean more than the basic information of when, where, and how long your talk is to be.

After-dinner, job-description and family talks can be more of a problem. The most obvious kind of talk, however, and the one we will have in mind for the rest of this section, is the afternoon or evening talk given to a mixed group of people in the church hall, village institute, school, or community centre. It may even be given after a meal. The audience size may vary and the thrust of what you are wanting to say will obviously be different depending on the audience, but it is crucial that you have a clear picture in your own mind of exactly what kind of a talk is expected from you.

Why me?

The reason you have been asked to give the talk now needs some examination. If you are a minister or vicar this may be obvious, but not always. Why have *you* been asked to speak? Might it be simply because there is nobody else? Or is it because your expertise is expected or well known? You should have an idea in the way the invitation came to you.

Frequently I have asked myself the question "What am I doing here?" Surrounded by a completely secular audience, clouded in cigarette smoke with more than enough empty wine bottles on the tables, is enough to make anyone ask such a question.

Whatever you do, work this out in your mind beforehand and do not verbalize it at the start of your talk. You will immediately alienate a small (or even large) percentage of your audience if you begin by saying "Now I am not qualified to be here but..." or "I don't know why I have been asked to give this talk but..." You must know this or you would not have agreed to be there!

When is it?

It is important that you know exactly when you are expected to give the talk. If it is part of a day conference with other speakers present, you should never be happy with "we'll give you a time nearer the date". This often results in confusion. If a date, place, and time are not made clear when you are asked to speak, make sure that you do not confirm the speaking engagement until it has all been organized. And then it should always be verified in writing. Missing a talk is really inexcusable if an audience has turned up expecting you, but you fail to arrive.

I remember once receiving a telephone call asking why I had not turned up at a certain mothers' union meeting only for them to discover between themselves that no one had actually invited me! The sudden feeling of horror that I had missed something I ought to have been at remained with me for some time. Know when you are giving a talk, where it is, and what time it will start. Always arrive at least ten minutes early to weigh up the auditorium. If you are preaching, it should be even earlier.

It is not a good idea to move into the pulpit during the service not having done so before. Make sure you stand in the pulpit before the service starts. On one occasion I did not do this and found to my horror that a false floor put in for the deacon (who was less than 5' 2") the week before had not been removed. It was definitely a case of the towering inferno! Check that you know where the light switch is and that the lectern is suitable for your needs. Also check for steps so that you do not fall into or out of the pulpit. If there is a microphone, feel free to adjust it; however,

MUMBLE, MUMBLE, MUMBLE, MUTTER, MUTTER!

do not put your mouth too close to it as this will result in distortion. If it is the preacher's job to turn the microphone on and off, remember to do both. If you are using a clip-on microphone make sure that you remember to leave it behind in the pulpit afterwards. I have seen some hilarious moments when, after a well-preached sermon, the minister has been exclusively remembered for the clip-on microphone that did a backward somersault as the next part of the service began.

It is also worthwhile checking when you should move to the pulpit. Very often, movement can be covered up neatly during a hymn or the singing of a psalm. It is best to move into the pulpit while something else is being done to help the flow of the service.

How long is it?

You cannot possibly prepare a talk unless you know how long you are expected to speak for. This does not mean that you cannot be flexible if something happens on the day to disrupt the original plans or if the event is running overtime. When you are booked to give a talk always establish how long you are expected to speak for and do not be content with "Well, whatever you think". It is just as bad to turn up with 30 minutes of good material to fill an hour as it is for an hour's talk that you will have to squeeze into 30 minutes.

Once you have been allocated a time, always aim for five minutes under that limit. This gives the audience the refreshing impression that you are in control of your material and not out to squeeze every allotted minute out of them. It is always good, if you are on the receiving end of a talk, when a speaker finishes early. We all appreciate a short sermon!

To write or not to write?

Many speakers know instinctively whether or not their talk will have to be written down. Sometimes this is determined by the nature of the address. If the organizers want "a text" there is no way of avoiding putting pen to paper — but very often it is a matter of style and confidence. Most speakers need at least prompt cards; some prefer to have the talk fully written out; others can manage without either — though the dangers of this are obvious.

Think carefully and realistically about your own command of the material, time, and your own memory. If you are to be accountable in any way for what you say (will there be a journalist present?), it is advisable to write down what some might call "the juicy bits". If your talk is primarily for entertainment it is much better to avoid a full script, as this can often result (and we have all witnessed this) in a laborious delivery. My own experience suggests that a series of key prompt-headings is more than sufficient for a relaxed and informative delivery. This conveys the impresson that you already have a good grasp of the subject-matter with which you are dealing, but that you have taken time to prepare carefully those parts of it that are in your talk.

Appearance

This is one area where television has affected people's expectations of how we look. It is important that you put some effort into looking reasonably smart, as people take particular note of your clothes, hair, shoes, and hands. People notice if a tie clashes with a shirt or if a particular hairstyle has changed, for better or for worse.

Before preaching a sermon or giving a talk, ask yourself if you look reasonably smart. I have seen many people taking services and preaching who look as if they have fallen out of bed and into the pulpit — a hairbrush can often do a great deal to remedy this.

So ask yourself: "Is there anything I can do to make myself less of a distraction so that what I want to say comes across simply?" One solution is to be as conservative or predictable in your dress as possible. I believe strongly that ministers should wear a clerical collar when delivering a talk because that is what an audience expects. Do you want them to spend the first ten minutes saying, "Is he *really* a Methodist minister?"

Laypeople can also score high marks for presentation by being soberly, yet attractively dressed. It may seem unimportant, but is in fact it is very important! Decide what to do with your briefcase or handbag before you enter a hall or room. Make sure you look and feel comfortable and avoid anything visual that will speak louder than your words.

Posture

If you are giving a talk you will usually be introduced by the chairman or president of the group or society that has invited you. It is useful to check that they know your name and position in the pre-chat before you stand up. As "Rob Marshall" I have been variously introduced as "Bob", "Rod", "Robin", and "Roy" Marshall!

When you eventually stand up to deliver your talk make sure that you will be comfortable, that you have enough room to stand, somewhere to put your notes, and that your posture is not distracting in any way. If you are preaching from a pulpit it may be a good idea to put any notes in the pulpit beforehand — as long as they are not moved before the service begins.

Do not fiddle with your glasses, and avoid unbuttoning and buttoning a handy button on your jacket. Try not to wave your hands around too much. Stand, lean a little on the lectern if you need to and, if the occasion is an appropriate one, smile — even if you do not feel like it! Keep your posture alert and convincing, and show the audience that you are enjoying yourself. Remember to smile!

Audience

By the time you actually stand up to deliver your talk you should have had time to weigh up your audience. I always find that this is one of the most fascinating aspects of preaching and giving talks. With experience, you can spot who the "nice ones" in the assembled gathering are and who might be the trouble-makers or cynics come question time. You can also detect who might nod off as soon as you open your mouth. I remember a recent dinner when I was being introduced by the president of a Round Table club. One chap had such a potentially bored look on his face that his seventeen-stone frame looked certain to doze off as soon as I stood up. Thus I consciously targeted him by looking at him throughout the talk (not continuously!) and to my amazement he stayed awake.

Is the congregation or audience what you anticipated? What about the twelve children under ten years of age that you did not expect? Is the audience closer or farther away from you than you thought?

It is crucially important that you establish a rapport with the gathering. Do not be a remote speaker, sounding off over their heads with words that they do not understand. You have come to talk *with* them. To each of them as individuals you are an expert on your subject and the general message you are sending out will be received by each in a different way.

Whether you are delivering a sermon, an informal talk in church, or the kind of talk we have been envisaging throughout most of this chapter, you must weigh up your audience at the start. Speak to them; communicate with them.

Choosing your words

If using the correct words is crucial when writing, it is equally important to choose the right words when you are giving a talk. We have all attended a talk or a lecture (and even more often, a sermon) where we have only understood 30 per cent of what was said — which often means that we understood nothing at all. A good communicator will use words and phrases that most people understand and will avoid terms that alienate the audience.

Christianity is littered with words that many people simply do not fathom (e.g. "ecumenical", "synod", "pentecost", "ascension"). If you want people to tune into what you are saying and stay listening, you have got to keep them with you by choosing words and phrases that inform and entertain. It can be an amusing exercise in itself to explain jargon words which will also allow you to show your expertise.

Visual aids

If your talk is longer than, say, fifteen minutes, it is useful to use some form of visual aid. This does not necessarily mean having a slide projector or a video. Simply producing an interesting item out of your pocket or a piece of paper from a nearby briefcase can help the listener change gear and continue moving smoothly along the road with you.

It is, however, vital not to overdo visual aids. If you want some good ideas you could try Paul Clowney's book *Picture It* (Bible Society, 1987). A National Audio Visual Aids Library is available at Paxton Place, Gipsy Road, London SE27 9SR.

If you are showing slides as part of a talk, use them sparingly and selectively. It is much better to show a few slides and entertain people rather than to force feed them with too many pictures that can only result in boredom. Ten slides that give a memorable and enduring impression are better than over a hundred that drive people to switch off completely.

Humour

The idea that you should always begin your talk or address with a funny story or a joke is a fallacy. Of course, it helps to relax the audience and can give them an appetite for more if they are "caught" or impressed by what you say in the opening stages. It is equally important to be natural, though, and not to tell jokes that are unlikely to work or offend people.

Humour in sermons is sometimes dangerous because of the possibility that it could backfire but, used well, it can add a great deal. I always feel that a funny story or a joke every so often does help the audience to "stay with you". More than two yawns from the same person is a definite indication that a funny story is urgently needed!

It is always better to tell anecdotes or jokes that have actually happened to you rather than repeating other people's stories. I have several horrendous memories of people struggling to find the punchline in badly rehearsed jokes that didn't work. Amusing real-life incidents will always go down better.

Audibility

This is obviously the most important aspect of any talk, whether you are giving it or listening. If people cannot hear what is being said then there is simply no point in saying it. If there is a reasonably effective microphone available, it is best to use it. Microphone technique will be discussed later in the chapter on radio, but the general rule is not to get too close to it. A distance of several inches between the microphone and the speaker is usually sufficient. There is nothing worse than a speaker who is spurting into a microphone with unnecessary noises accompanying the talk.

If necessary, ask the audience if they can hear you — this at least gets the two-way process of communication off to a good start. If, however, they say "no", you will have to be able to remedy the problem quickly otherwise it will be a pointless exercise.

Barriers

Before starting your talk it is important to analyse what barriers
will have to be broken down in order to communicate your points
effectively. In a sermon this is less likely to be a problem, but in a
talk to a predominantly secular group there can be a minefield to
negotiate. There are always going to be some barriers between you
and the audience.

The most obvious ones are distractions that are sometimes
unavoidable. Waiters or waitresses clearing tables after a dinner is
a common one, as are roadworks outside the building, or pan-
tomime practice in the room next door! If you as speaker are
affected by distractions, your audience will be as well. If the barrier is obvious, make a joke out of it at the start so that the audience knows that you are aware of it and that the distraction is not a
major problem for you.

Also, be aware of cultural and spiritual barriers that often exist
between "religious" speakers and some audiences. This is important in all other forms of Christian communication as well. Tuning
into the audience's wavelength involves being aware of the culture
in which they are based. Are they mainly home-owners who regularly play golf and hardly watch any television? Or are they mainly
down-to-earth people who like a pint and never miss a "soap"?
Such generalizations sound crude, but it is important that you
assess the cultural background of your audience.

Too many Christian speakers also create spiritual barriers by
talking about issues and subjects that mean absolutely nothing to
90 per cent of their audience. Do not presume too much. Weigh up
what barriers there are or might be between you and the audience
and then try to overcome them by establishing a rapport at the
right level.

Length of talk

Having discovered how long your talk should be, it is not a good
idea to exceed your limit. Indeed, as I stressed above, try and aim
to finish about five minutes within your allotted time (if your talk
is more than thirty minutes) and a couple of minutes within if it is
less than thirty minutes.

It is also important not to make constant references to the passing of time in your delivery. An occasional "time is moving on, so

I must get on with the next point" is fine, but the listener can do without such references every two minutes. This can give the impression of a series of shallow points which are skating over the surface.

Questions

If you have agreed to answer questions after your talk, be careful that your answers do not amount to a supplementary address. Be clear, direct, and concise; and refer in your answer to the question asked. Limit any answer to not more than a couple of minutes. If you know that a meeting has to finish at 2.00 p.m. and the chair-person asks for any questions at 2.03 p.m., any favourable impression you have made in the talk will evaporate if you continue to give long answers to questions that should not really have been asked because time had run out.

And finally...

Obviously, it is not possible to take on board all the points that I have raised when turning up to give a simple talk to a harmless-looking group on a cold March evening. Some might even protest that we are, after all, talking about the Christian Church and not a super-organized industry. The expectations of our audiences are, however, very real indeed and we can all improve our interpersonal communication so that the message of Jesus may be more clearly heard.

Whatever our starting point, the ultimate aim should be the same. The power of speech is obvious and it should be used to maximum effect when the occasion demands it in preaching or speaking. Whether preaching, giving a short informal talk, an important after-dinner speech, or a cosy afternoon chat in the local village hall, it really is a communications challenge that we can all respond to. If we develop and improve our interpersonal communication, our work in the other areas that we shall now look at is bound to improve as well.

A WAY WITH WORDS

We have to look for what someone has called a prose for God and it may be that we shall be best served by reading, not learned and abstract theological works, but nursery stories, folktales, the classical myths and above all the Bible.
(T. Rowe)

The ability to write in a clear, concise, and easily understood style is not a skill that everybody has. Yet effective writing skills are essential in today's world if we want to make contact with people. Here, I am not concerned with specialist Christian writers who have their books published. Rather, I am interested in the average church community where things need to be written down. Parish magazines, Sunday newsletters, committee minutes, and press releases very often tend to be written in a language that few people outside the Church actually understand. Here we need to bear in mind the internal/external argument of our opening chapter.

The central question is — what are people used to reading (e.g. newspapers (broadsheet or tabloid?), magazines, leaflets, or novels?) in their everyday lives, and how can we best provide written material in our churches that is attractive, informative, and professionally presented so that it can further the spreading of the gospel?

TABLOID TRENDS

The strength and emergence of tabloid newspapers and the hundreds of magazines that flood the market every week and month has greatly affected the average reader's reading habits. If you study the written media carefully, you will see that most newspapers, and not only the tabloids, now use very short paragraphs and equally short sentences.

Most of the weekend newspapers also have supplements, magazines and pull-out sections. These rely, as the tabloid press have always done, on concise sentences and paragraphs. Anything that departs remotely from such a well-established style (i.e. long paragraphs, tedious sentences, difficult words) will immediately be seen as irrelevant and boring because this is not what most people are used to. Even the broadsheet newspapers like *The Times* and the *Independent* have established a simple, direct style based on short paragraphs and the economic use of language.

JESUS WROTE NOTHING DOWN

All models of Christian communication are rooted ultimately in the words and works of Jesus; his simple and direct style was the hallmark of his whole ministry. However, Jesus himself did not record anything in written form that we know of. As the Gospel writers discovered after the resurrection, any attempt to record Jesus' words and deeds in writing results in numerous problems. This book is not about the complex subject of oral and written traditions in the New Testament; it is enough here to note that the writing down of Jesus' words and deeds did not prove an easy exercise for the early Church.

Explaining in written form the significance of the Word made flesh was, nevertheless, the task of the evangelists — those who tried to preserve the good news for future generations. It also remains the responsibility of all those who write as Christians today. We see the early Church, and particularly St Paul, dealing with the new images, concepts, and values that Jesus had brought into being. Words such as "follow", "righteousness", "kingdom", and "remembrance" took on a new meaning. Thus a new vocabulary, both spoken and written, emerged.

To those who believed, the language was an exciting discovery. However, to those who remained outside the Church, a communications barrier was immediately brought into being. In order that someone might believe in the Word it had to become real and intelligible to them, and yet we have vast pockets of the population who are unable to read and write, from the time of Jesus until now, and thus fail to grasp the truth that Jesus came to share.

Eddie Gibbs (in *The God Who Communicates,* Hodder & Stoughton) summed this up very simply when he concluded that Christianity "is couched in the language which Christians use to address one another rather than translated into a vocabulary which is intelligible, and into thought forms which are relevant to the world beyond the church frontiers" (p. 20). When we write we have to find words that people actually understand. In all forms of written and spoken communication we must be aware of the context in which we are placed. We have to speak and to write *for* people.

WHAT DO WE FIND?

Today's churches are full of specialized language and jargon — just read any parish magazine, fellowship-group minutes, synod agenda or minister's letter! Anyone who is not acquainted with church life will tell you that church issues and politics are often more difficult to understand than local government, cricket or an income-tax return form. Also, this is not only the case when it comes to church news, politics, and issues. Church worship is full of words, phrases, and images that the vast majority of people do not understand ("the body and blood of Jesus", "calvary", "sing some choruses", "confirmation", "intercessions"). I frequently look at the faces of occasional worshippers (Christmas Eve congregations, baptism families, and funeral gatherings) and it is obvious that the words are generally conveying nothing to them and that the language needs explaining.

Writing about the life of the Church is a problem faced by clergy and laity alike. Ministers, for instance, when writing a pastoral letter to the community, often find the transition from university or theological college to writing for the average person in the pew a communications bridge that is difficult to cross. It is also true that members of the laity (people who are doctors, labourers, accountants, teachers and nurses throughout the week) find writing about the Christian faith in a language that most people understand extremely difficult, if not impossible.

Some writing published by clergy for the public domain is unintelligible. Other contributions are interesting as far as the subject-matter is concerned, but the style and diction is complicated and boring. I have a copy of a well-produced, desktop-published parish magazine in front of me which looks pretty good at first sight. However, when I started to read it I discovered that the first paragraph of the vicar's letter has fourteen sentences in it and contains several words that the average person will not understand ("ecumenical approach"; "the stewards' focus appeal" "UPA parish"). The contribution from the headteacher of the church school is equally complicated. It is all about "LMS" (Local Management of Schools, which is never explained) while the stewardship committee chairperson stresses that she is concerned about the finances of the parish in an opening paragraph that beats the vicar's in that it has seventeen sentences! The magazine is littered with names, abbreviations, and events that are never explained ("MU", "TAP", "vestry meeting", "Spring Harvest", etc.). I'm sure such examples will be very familiar to you. The danger is of creating the impression of an exclusive club rather than a missionary church. Thus how we write things down is crucial.

I have mountains of evidence to prove my case further, having for many years been a diocesan communications officer serving bishops, cathedrals, clergy, laity, and parishes. People who are part of the Church find writing about the gospel extremely difficult. As editor of the Bradford diocesan newspaper (*Newsround*) for over four years (a typical in-house, tabloid journal reaching 16,000 churchgoers), I often commissioned stories and articles from clergy and laity alike. I am now on the receiving end of the same kind of material in the Diocese of London.

Frequently, I would ask a contributor for a 500-word article or a 200-word news story. Equally often, they would deliver an 800-word article and a 350-word news story! Sometimes articles would exceed their requested length by more than 300 per cent and were written in what can only be described as a foreign language, using incomprehensibe words, long sentences, and a laborious style. If the editor has to search through a dictionary to understand the meaning, then the chances of the average reader understanding the piece are probably nil.

Regardless of who you are writing for, the language has to be as simple and direct as possible in all forms of writing aimed at an average readership. So, from the outset, you need to ask who you are writing for. As we stressed in the opening chapter, always ask the basic question: "Is this is for internal or external consumption?"

Unfortunately this question is rarely asked before the writing is started. I remember one Yorkshire town council of churches circulating 5,000 leaflets through the doors of a housing estate, urging people to "come to our ecumenical service". Someone joked that people might think it was for the launch of the European Ecu in the village. Another Anglican church invited members of the parish via their posters to come to their "Patronal Festival". If what you are writing is mainly for the wider (and not church) community, it is important to make extra sure that people will understand.

Having established who your audience is, we now turn to some practical guidelines. First we need to make another basic point about people's expectations with regard to style, for an awareness of lack of understanding of church terminology and issues is only the start. Many will say that it is the task of the Christian Church to set standards; even, perhaps, standards of literacy. However, there is no point in trying to communicate the gospel unless we take seriously the context in which that communication takes place. It is for this reason that a popular style with simple vocabulary and short paragraphs is the order of the day.

BASIC GUIDELINES FOR POPULAR WRITING

Purpose

It is important to establish the purpose behind the piece of writing you are about to undertake. Is it to inform, educate, entertain or to convert? Why are you writing what you are writing? Do you know what the start, middle, and end of the piece is?

I usually read over one hundred parish magazines a month and am convinced that many contributors simply sit down and write their contributions without any regard for the actual purpose behind their writing. Have a goal in mind and aim for it from the start.

Length

Always have an idea about how long a piece of writing is going to be when you begin. An average sheet of double-spaced A4 paper is about 250 words. As I stated above, clergy and laity are both equally guilty of being unable to stick to a required length which is either obvious from a previous format or specified by the editor. This is a basic requirement.

If you are writing for a journal or magazine other than your own, it is courteous to stick to the limit you have been given. If you find that, despite all your attempts to keep to the limit, you are still a little over, be ruthless with a pen or the delete key on your word processor.

The ultimate offender here was a request for 2,000 words of copy for a major feature in a diocesan newspaper centre-spread. I actually received, as editor, over 12,000 words! Copies abound of various parish magazines where the vicar's letter continues for more than the required length. Some simply don't know when to stop. A rough guide here is to suggest that parish-magazine articles should never exceed 600 words and that 400 is usually enough.

Vocabulary

As I have already emphasized, it is important to use short words that are easily understood. Avoid technical jargon (e.g. "eschatological", "ecumenical", "catechumens", "christological") that alienates the reader. The more you can say in a direct, understandable manner, the greater the chance that your reader will be impressed by what you have written down.

There is always an alternative to a longer or technical word and here a *Roget's Thesaurus* or synonym finder is invaluable. In written statements to the press, avoid colloquialisms and clichés ("at all costs", "if you see what I mean", "like the plague") that sound absurd when quoted in a written format. Keep it simple.

Style

Much of what is important here has already been mentioned. Take into account the context in which you are writing and what other journals and newspapers your audience will be reading. The writing should not appear "churchy" or difficult. Everyone will write in their own particular style, but there are some basic guidelines to bear in mind. The evangelists help us here. Each of the four Gospel writers attempt to explain exactly the same story in very different ways and thus adopt varying styles. Similarly, today's journalists reporting the same event, will use different styles.

Keep your paragraphs short; in popular writing no paragraph should contain more than three sentences. Avoid complicated sentence constructions like this one from a recent London parish magazine:

> *The Christmas Eve Celebrations begin at 4 p.m. with the Blessing of the Crib which will be followed by a Midnight Mass beginning at 11 p.m. which actually begins our Christmas celebrations though you have other opportunities to come to Communion at 8 a.m., 9 a.m. and 12 noon when said services will take place though children will be welcome at all of them.*

The above paragraph can easily be given a more punchy style with a little care and thought.

Rudolph Flesch (in *The Art of Readable Writing*, Collier-Macmillan, 1962) urged us to "Use short words — 150 syllables per 100 words; short sentences — no more than nineteen words per sentence. Human interest should be at the rate of 6 per cent names, personal pronouns or words referring to people or having masculine or feminine gender." Such basic advice on style should be taken very seriously. We can now turn to some practical examples: a parish-magazine article, a press release, and writing committee minutes.

.... FULL STOP. NEW PARAGRAPH. CAPITAL ROMAN 'T' WITH DECORATIVE GILT EDGING AROUND IT.

KEEPING IT SIMPLE

The flood of images which pours from the mass media ensures that everyone is able to find those images which most resonate with their own experience, in the process confirming and affirming those beliefs and experiences. (D. Weber, *Discerning Images,* Edinburgh University Press, 1991.)

Many of the basic principles highlighted in the previous chapter need to be applied to all forms of written communication. The *context* is crucial; the *aim* should be obvious; the *style* needs to be as simple as possible.

Most churches have a regular magazine or weekly newsheet and an increasing number have both. Church publicity documents are notoriously difficult to understand if you approach them as an outsider. Many churches try to address the regular attenders and the wider community with limited success. Such publications do not usually replace verbal notices before, during or after a service. It is a way of giving people something to take away to reinforce what they have been told verbally, though some ministers no longer read out such notices and rely exclusively on the noticesheet.

THE WEEKLY BULLETIN

Travelling around and visiting churches in the course of my work is very revealing when you try, as a stranger, to understand some of the noticesheets that you are given when you go into a church. These usually contain the date, service titles, hymns, notices for the week ahead, and other little clips from life in the church. The quality of them varies a great deal.

Some names and words are not explained and abbreviations are overused. Although such newsletters are an internal form of communication, they should be comprehensible to anyone who might visit you on Sunday. The inadequate way services are explained, the lack of surnames, and the general feeling that the weekly newsletter is for those who are "in the know" should be guarded against. Always keep it simple and explain as much as you can.

Name of church and date

Is it a special Sunday? If so, say something about it. Don't leave people guessing!

Be friendly

Help people to find their way in the services

Is there a guest preacher? Say who he or she is

Say <u>when</u> and <u>where</u> weekly events are taking place

Who is the contact person for events?

HOLY TRINITY CHURCH, ANYTOWN

Sunday 4 June   **Pentecost Sunday**

A very warm welcome to everyone who joins us for worship today. After the 10.00 a.m. service, there will be refreshments and a chance to meet other members of the congregation informally. Do join us!

Pentecost Sunday is a day of thanksgiving in the Christian calendar when we celebrate the sending of the Holy Spirit to the first disciples of Jesus, after he had risen from the dead.

TODAY'S SERVICES

8.00 a.m. <u>HOLY COMMUNION</u>
You will find the Order of Service on page 7 of the small orange booklets.

10.00 a.m. <u>FAMILY SERVICE</u>
Guest Preacher: The Bishop of St James's Park, the Rt Revd Dr Eric Sharples.

Today's hymns: 86, 29, 562, 73

Bible Reading: Acts 2.1–11

WHAT'S ON THIS WEEK?

<u>Monday 5 June</u>
7.30 p.m. Mothers' Union Annual General Meeting in the Church Hall. New members always welcome. Contact Sybil Walty (tel. 665231).

<u>Tuesday 6 June</u>
2.00 p.m. Mums' and toddlers' group in the Church Hall. Contact Trudy Moody (tel. 676473).

Many bulletins are now produced on a word processor and some parishes use desk-top publishing. The appearance of these productions is usually excellent. Some use a typewriter and then photocopy, while others still resort to the ink duplicator. There are obvious advantages and disadvantages to all forms of production, but matters of style, content, finance, and resources are all relevant. There are many examples we could give here of written documents in church life, but to help focus our attention we will concentrate on three of the most common ones.

WRITING FOR A CHURCH MAGAZINE

As stressed continually in the previous chapter, it is important to remember the influence of tabloid journalism on people's reading expectations. Most churches have some kind of magazine or newsletter that is read by its members and others in the community. The quality of these varies enormously. Later we shall concern ourselves with the presentation and layout of such publications, but for the moment we will concentrate on the content. Remember that the weekly newsletter is for internal consumption, while the church magazine is read by those in the wider community. A basic summary of aims and objectives can help us here.

The contents of the average parish magazine are highly predictable. Most of them have a cover, a directory of names and telephone numbers, a minister's comment, news from the uniformed organizations, youth and other societies, and lists of rotas. The vast majority of these publications are monthly, but some appear bimonthly and others on a quarterly basis.

You may be asked to write:

- a pastoral letter;
- a report of an event;
- an obituary;
- an appeal;
- a feature-type article.

The frequency of the publication and the copy-deadlines are important because of the author's need to be up to date and relevant. Parish magazines should not be (though most are) summaries of what took place in the church some six weeks ago. Always try to ask yourself the following questions:

When will it be published?

Before writing a contribution it is necessary to establish when the magazine will actually be published and read. It is then important to take this into account when writing about the spring fair, the school governors or Christmas services. Some magazine editors have a policy of asking contributors to be proactive in their copy. This means spending three lines on what has already happened and the rest on what is about to happen in the month of publication. Although this is not always easy, it gives the publication a futuristic feel and stops people from gaining the impression that the magazine has come out of a time warp.

Who will read it?

Most church magazines are read by a combination of churchgoers and people who have absolutely nothing to do with the church; the latter sometimes buy it to show some form of unattached association with the work of the local Christian community. As a curate in Leeds I would often do funeral visits and spot, out of the corner of my eye, the parish magazine on the coffee table — even though the deceased and the surviving relatives had never set foot in the church.

If this is the case, the contribution you are writing must take into account those who are generally ignorant of church life and language. As we have already stressed it is essential to avoid in-words, abbreviations, and code words that people do not understand. It is possible, but not at all easy, to achieve a balance and a language that speaks to both regular attenders and those who do not come to church services.

Getting your facts right

Once you know who you are writing for and when it will appear, you need to make sure that your information is correct. Church life is often littered with misinformation — wrong dates, inaccurate times, incorrect titles and general misunderstandings. A good example of this is the Harvest Supper starting at 7.30 p.m. in the parish magazine...7.45 p.m. in the weekly newsheet and 8 p.m. on the posters. I myself have been guilty of many such errors!

Who is it from

Start with something that people are going to identify with

Ask questions and engage the reader

Express yourself simply

Use short paragraphs

Explain jargon, if you <u>must</u> use it

Tell people where they can find details or information

End by making a connection with your beginning

FROM THE MINISTER

Are you a soap addict? No, I'm not talking about someone who slips off to the bathroom for a frothy, bubbly bath at every opportunity. I'm talking about someone who is "hooked" on soap operas like *Coronation Street* or *Eastenders*. Well, I certainly am! In fact — between me and you — I try to avoid any meetings when these programmes are on, just in case I miss something important as the story unfolds.

Why is it that soap operas have this power to captivate and hold our attention?

One of the reasons is that the story line and the characters speak to our own situation in such a vivid way. We are able to identify ourselves as we watch the characters totter from one disaster to another, as they celebrate their good fortunes, and come to terms with disappointment and tragedy. "All of life is there".

I often wonder whether the writers of the Bible, had they lived in our own age, would have approved of soaps. The writers of the Gospels, in particular, seem to want to draw us into the story-line as they recall the events of Jesus' life and death. We can see ourselves in the characters and events.

As we come together to celebrate the events in Jesus' life that recall his last week on earth (known as Holy Week), it is important that we see ourselves in that story. These events are just as important for us today.

On page 12 of this month's edition of *Church News* you will find details of all the services during Holy Week. I hope that all of us will take the opportunity to worship during this week and use it to involve ourselves in the drama of Jesus' life, death, and resurrection.

You never know, watching soap operas, as well as reading the Bible, may help us to do this more effectively — especially if we can see ourselves more clearly in them both.

Rod Sherrif

Just as important, though, is ensuring that information in articles is accurate. Community politics are a minefield and it is wise to check your facts. Is Mr Jenkins really Stan and not Sam? Did Mrs Limehouse step down as president in 1990 or 1992? With all these things in mind you are now ready to write!

The writing itself

To recap, keep it simple, and always stick to the length that has been agreed beforehand. Write in short sentences, using words that people will understand and keep the paragraphs concise. There should be no more than three or four sentences in each paragraph. In a local church it is a good idea to relate your piece to the home situation. People love to see their names (or better still their children's names!), streets, organizations, or friends in print. Be as topical as you can and try and make the reader eager to read what you are about to write. Have an opening, a beginning, and an ending. If possible, split the text up a little by using sub-headings, and make sure that you are consistent in your use of capitals and abbreviations ("Diocese/diocese", "Revd/Rev"). It all adds up to a neater and more effective finished product.

There are numerous publications to give you further help in this area. The best recent publication is undoubtedly John Coles's *How to Produce a Parish Magazine* (Rattlesden, Palm Tree Press, 1989).

NEWS RELEASES

A news release is a method by which you inform the local media of an event or a happening that you believe is news. They are widely used by many companies and organizations to communicate news to various forms of media, but in church life they are not used enough. As far as issuing news releases as part of a proactive strategy is concerned, many people are reluctant even to contemplate such a process. Many churches are generally concerned about what a newspaper or radio station might do with their story and so they avoid communicating news.

When we decide to issue a news release we need to do as professional a job as we can. Most church events would concentrate almost exclusively on the local press, but there may be the occasional happening that might gain national exposure. The church newspapers and magazines are always on the look out for new material.

If you were to spend a week in any local newspaper office you would see that news releases come in from a wide variety of organizations — schools, local businesses, sports clubs, Rotary Clubs, WIs and a whole host of others. Some are well produced, while others are appalling. The majority are typed, but some are hand-written.

You would see some on reasonable notepaper, and others on bits of cardboard or scraps of paper. So what is the best way of going about drawing the attention of the press to an event that we want publicity for?

Here is a basic guide to producing news releases:

- A news release must contain news: no newspaper editor is going to be interested in pure advertising; you are expected to pay for that. There has to be an event, a person, an issue that is newsworthy. The news will need to be offered in a lively, stimulating, and exciting way.

- Find out what people in your church and immediate area rely on for local news. Make a composite list of all media outlets. This will include the local newspapers (paid for and free), local radio, and your local television newsroom. It may be worth sending the release to your own church denominational newspaper. Send your press releases to everyone on your main list on all occasions — so that they actually become used to receiving them. They will then be recognized and you will gain the respect of the news-rooms.

- Use easily identifiable notepaper; it is best to have some specially printed. Usually the mast head should contain some kind of drawing or logo along with the name of the organization and, in bold letters, the words "News Release". Such stationery can be printed cheaply at a local community printers. Remember that if you use colour when printing the stationery you have to put the sheets into a photocopier, whereas black and white artwork can be photocopied directly on to blank paper.

- Remember the copy deadlines for the media outlets. Most local newspapers are weekly and are published on a Friday; they usually need copy by the previous Wednesday morning. Evening regional papers need a story before 9.30 a.m. Local radio usually have religious programmes on Sundays which are put together on Thursdays and Fridays. If you have a big event at a weekend, it is imperative that you have the news release out by a Tuesday evening .

- At the top of the news release it is important that you state when the information can be used. If it can be used at any time simply write "For Immediate Use" alongside the date. If, however, the material is being released before an event, you will need to embargo the information. This means writing "Strictly Embargoed Until 1400 on Thursday 23 October 1997" and a reporter will respect the fact that you have supplied information that can be reported only after the time stated. This is particularly useful when it comes to speeches and sermons.

- As well as a date and directions for usage, it is also a good idea to give each news release an eye-catching title. "Minister to Visit Nepal" or "Nepal Visit" will immediately grab the journalist's attention. Do not simply send off the text without providing a catchline heading.

- We now come to the most important part of a news release: the opening paragraph. In a few words you need to summarize what the news release is all about. You must explain *what* is happening, *who* is involved, *where* it is, *when* it is, and *why* the event is taking place. All of this should be included in the opening sentence. Do not ramble off into a complicated, longwinded explanation. Attempt to grab the journalist's attention by using a turn of phrase that stands out: "Portsmouth welcomes the Archbishop of Canterbury on Saturday 23 April as the guest speaker at a special rally in Pearson Park organized by local churches (7.30 p.m.)". The rest of the news release involves unpacking the information contained in the opening paragraph.

- The language of news releases needs a great deal of careful thought. Remember that the reporter reading your text may just have read one from the local council and another from the police press office. You have to avoid words that mean little or nothing to a secular journalist. You should use a lively, punchy style. No paragraph should contain more than two sentences — standard practice in most newspaper writing. Make sure that sentences are short and to the point. If a sentence is too long, break it up into two. Keep the text short; seven paragraphs is more than enough.

- The layout of news releases is very important because of the visual impression created. Always leave a gap between the lines so that a reporter can sub-edit your story. In other words, they may want to insert the odd word or scribble bits underneath. It is also usual practice to photocopy news releases on one side only, so avoid putting page 2 (if there is one!) on the back of page 1. It should be on a separate sheet.

- News releases should always have a contact name and daytime telephone number at the end of the script. The person listed should be fully briefed about all aspects of the event and should be able to assist the journalist in whatever way is necessary. Never send out news releases without a contact person.

If you follow these basic guidelines, you will be amazed at how much more notice the media will take of even a fairly average event. Sending out well-presented, short and attractive news releases on a regular basis establishes good relationships with the local media.

We deal with the whole question of media liaison in a later chapter but there are two other important points that need to be mentioned here in conjunction with the sending out of News Releases: photographs and press conferences.

Who is it from?

What is it?

Has it been embargoed or is it for immediate use?

Always give the date

Short, eye-catching headline

Say what it is; where it is; when it is; and why it is happening
in the first paragraph

Use short paragraphs

Give details of the main subject

Say something about the idea

How will it happen?

Has a local leader given support to the event?

Say when the information ends

Who can give further details?

HOLY TRINITY CHURCH, ANYTOWN

NEWS RELEASE

For Immediate Use   3 August 2003

"WORLD RECORD ATTEMPT"

A sponsored 48-hour hymn-singing marathon is to take place in Holy Trinity Church, Anytown, at 7.00 p.m. on Friday 14 August, to raise £5,000 towards sending thirteen-year-old Sarah Philips to the USA for a life-saving operation.

Sarah, chorister at Holy Trinity Church, suffers from a rare blood disorder and needs an urgent operation that is not available in the UK.

The event is the idea of the church organist, Henry Clegg. He discovered that the existing world record for a non-stop hymn-singing session stands at 36 hours.

"I know that we could beat it," he said. "Sarah is held in such affection, and everyone is determined to help," he added.

Members of the church will be approaching local people for sponsorship over the next two weeks, and inviting anyone to pop into the church and join in with the singing over the weekend.

Councillor Mrs Joan Trimble, Mayor of Anytown, gave the project her wholehearted support. "It's a tremendous effort which will help Sarah and put our town into the record books," she said.

ENDS

Further information from either Henry Clegg (Daytime Tel. 672341 or Evening Tel. 457821)

or the Vicar of Holy Trinity, the Revd Ken Trend (Tel. 602378).

Photographs

Most local newspapers are always on the lookout for good picture stories. They will usually ring you up, having read your news release, and ask if they can come and take a picture.

If you agree to this you have to bear several points in mind. First, if an event is starting at 7.30 p.m. do not arrange for the photographer to come then. Insist that he comes at least thirty minutes before the event or at the end. Secondly, think about picture possibilities; church groups of confirmation candidates with the bishop, or old ladies on an outing appear every week in most local newspapers, so try and think of something new.

Think of a good picture and suggest it. If the photographer comes up with an idea be cautious that you are not being "set up" for a picture you do not want but, at the same time, he may have exactly the right idea. Always beware of a photographer who comes armed with a visual aid to emphasize a particular point (like a giant door-key for the "Canon Locks Out Thieves" story or a pair of theatrical wings to put on the back of the "Choirgirl of the year"). Remember, a picture can speak louder than words at times.

Press conferences

Reporters are no longer out and about in the community in the way that they were years ago. The telephone is the main method of obtaining information. There is, therefore, no point in calling a press conference unless it is absolutely necessary.

If a new building is opening or a very famous person is visiting, you may invite the local media for an informal meeting before the actual event. But press conferences should be used sparingly and, if your denomination has a local press officer, it is best to ask for expert help and advice.

WRITING MINUTES FOR GROUPS AND COMMITTEES

Churches tend to have more than their fair share of committees, groups, and organizations where a record of their proceedings needs to be kept.

Minute writing is an important art whether we are talking about a church council, a school governing body, or the youth group support team.

...AND NOW OVER TO OUR SECRETARY WHO HAS A SUMMARY OF
THE MINUTES FROM OUR LAST P.C.C. MEETING!

Minutes often tend to be too long and emphasize points and arguments that need not be recorded. The purpose of minutes is generally to give a concise and accurate record of what went on and that which was finally decided at a meeting.

Have you ever stopped to think about who will actually use the minutes you are writing? It is possible they may be used in future years, but generally only by people who want to check up on decisions of policy and finance. In my experience, church minutes tend to be too long and overstate discussion, policy, and conclusions. In this age of crisp, clear communication we can all be more concise and economical without sacrificing accuracy and detail.

SOUND WORDS

If you want to air your faith, you should first get to know something about the air. (E. Robertson, *Air Your Faith,* Jay Books, 1991.)

We come now to the world of radio. Over the past few years there has been a tremendous number of changes in the world of radio ranging from the BBC World Service, through to national radio and the many local radio stations broadcasting across the country. The number of radio stations has dramatically increased and millions of people are still listening to this medium. The need for religion to be represented at all levels in radio remains a great challenge to regular broadcasters and those of us who are called upon to contribute from time to time.

Without doubt radio is my favourite form of media, and yet a radio interview can be a very difficult experience. You cannot be seen, and your interviewer is not visible. Listeners are easily distracted by many other things and there is a danger that you simply become background noise. Despite this, in its own way, radio can be much more revealing than television because it focuses the attention on the spoken word, rather like a sermon. The only difference is that it is easier to shut the person up by switching off the radio!

Radio is more immediate than other forms of media. An announcement can be made as it happens, and nothing visual is required. Hence radio's preoccupation at local level with traffic news, weather, school closures, racing results, and news from the share markets. Also, radio is a very portable form of media — you can listen in the car, in the garden, and even via a personal stereo radio as you sit, wait, or walk (with caution!)

WHICH RADIO?

Radio audiences often peak in the age range of 16–34, but the numbers listening to the radio have been increasing in all age groups since 1984 (*UK Factfile,* Michael O'Mara Books, 1990). Radio listening now stands on average at nine hours and twelve minutes a week for all age groups.

Radio is far more popular in the morning than at any other time of the day with 15.5 per cent of the population listening to a radio station between 8.00 a.m. and 8.30 a.m. This, however, contrasts markedly with the 40.3 per cent who are watching television between 9.00 p.m. and 9.30 p.m. In any one week, though, 74 per cent of the population will tune in their radio sets.

These statistics remind us that radio remains an important means of making contact with people. However, we do need to be aware of the different types of radio station currently available in most regions before we agree to make a contribution or to seek publicity from them.

The BBC has five national stations, all of which have a particular remit as far as their content is concerned. It is possible to state broadly that Radio 1 attracts much younger listeners than Radio 3; Radio 5 is primarily for sport and education; Radio 2 deals with "middle-of-the road" music; and Radio 4 is almost entirely speech-based. Independent radio is also moving into the national network now.

As far as the churches are concerned, our main contact with the world of radio will be very much at local level. BBC local radio began in 1967 when BBC Radios Leicester, Sheffield and Merseyside came on the air; they were eventually followed by dozens of others that covered the whole country. Independent local radio followed in 1969 and competition obviously increased. In recent years commercial stations have been splitting frequencies to create even more stations and there has been the regionalization of BBC local stations for evening and weekend listening.

This has serious implications for the churches. First, the possibility of representatives being asked to contribute to a programme as a representative of a church, group, or organization is more likely now than ever before. It is also true that changes in the ecumenical scene mean that greater financial and resources co-operation is now needed if the churches are to maintain their current level of involvement in local radio.

Most local radio stations begin their Sunday morning output with a two-hour breakfast show which usually reflects the local religious life. It is obvious from the feedback to these programmes that the audience consists largely of non-churchgoers. After years of involvement in local radio in the north of England, I have discovered that most ministers do not listen to local radio while laypeople do. Also, people who do not normally go to church want to hear religious argument and discussion. This secular audience also likes hymns and religious music.

The possibilities are enormous, but there are also standards and expectations that the audience presume. So it is important that all of us who are at any time involved in radio do what we can to present the gospel in a simple and effective way.

So let us turn to the practical side of being involved in the world of radio. Either you have sent off one of your news releases as discussed in the last chapter and the telephone has rung, or the radio station has contacted you for help. What are they expecting?

TYPES OF CONTRIBUTION

The interview

Most people are invited to contribute to a radio station by being interviewed and much of the advice offered below is about such a situation. Obviously, it is important to prepare well for any interview in relation to the words that you will use. This usually involves going into a studio and being chatted to by an experienced presenter or producer.

You will need to overcome the effect that the microphone, studio, and other people hanging around might have on you.

The interview on location

This is almost the same as the interview mentioned above, but this time the radio station comes to you with a tape recorder to do the interview where you are. It is also possible to record an interview on the telephone. Both these types of interview require more care and attention than the studio interview simply because you will sound more distant and there is a greater possibility of you being distracted.

The panel discussion

Local radio stations often like to create panel discussions to debate a whole variety of different issues and subjects, and you will often be just one voice among many on such a panel. This is a very different experience to the straightforward interview and demands a definite motivation on your part. You must *want* to contribute.

Set-script contribution

Much traditional Christian broadcasting still centres on the "Thought for the Day" or "Pause for Thought" contribution. Local radio maintains a special interest in such contributions, although these days there is a greater multi-faith emphasis.

The need here is to combine writing and broadcasting skills so that the material sounds fresh, original, and not churchy. However, it is a very different experience sitting in a studio delivering a script as opposed to being asked questions.

We now turn to a step-by-step guide to dealing with a radio challenge.

Who and what?

Most approaches, whether proactive or reactive, will come to you from the radio station via the telephone. You may well be contacted at very short notice and asked to contribute. Frequently a radio station will ring and ask you to do a telephone interview immediately, or to come in later that morning. If the request is for a weekend religious programme, you may have notice of a day or more.

Once the request has been made by the radio station for an interview, it is important that you consider it carefully. If the issue is important to you and the publicity is necessary, you may have to make room for the interview in an already crowded timetable.

Find out who is talking to you on the telephone and jot down their name. Is it a researcher, the presenter, or the producer? Always ask if anyone else will be taking part in the interview. If you are to give one side of an argument, ask who will be giving the other. Will you be debating on air or will you be interviewed separately? Make sure you know what you are being asked to do. Make a note of the name of the programme.

Studio or telephone?

As we have already mentioned, there are three main methods of contributing to a radio station. The first, and by far the best, is "live" in the studio. To be in the same place as the interviewer gives you an obvious advantage. As a frequent contributor to the "Pause for Thought" slot on Radio 2, I am more than aware of the advantage of actually being in the studio with the presenter rather than somewhere else. Other alternatives include a local studio close to your home from where you can be linked up by a line to the main studio, or a telephone interview.

If you are unable to go to the main studio, but can go to the local one always do so. The advantage of a local studio is that the sound quality of your voice will be as good as in the main studio. In fact the listeners will not know that you are not with the presenter. The telephone interview is always inferior because you could just as well be in Tangiers or Tel Aviv as in Tottenham.

Live or recorded?

Some of the biggest laughs I have had as a local radio presenter have come from seeing people's faces when they arrive at a studio on a Sunday morning and suddenly realize that what they are going to say will go out live on air. "You mean I can't make any mistakes? Is it really live?" I remember a member of one young wives' group arriving one Sunday and almost refusing to go on.

SO KEN YOUR MARRIAGE IS ON THE VERGE OF A BREAKDOWN...
I'M SORRY BUT I CAN'T REALLY HELP YOU THERE!

The simple fact was that she had not asked the basic question: "will it be recorded or will it be live?"

Live pieces are always the best; they are more human and allow you to be more yourself. Recorded interviews are dangerous in that they are often much longer than the final piece that will eventually be broadcast and therefore there will be some editorial cutting which may destroy the natural flow of the conversation — or, worse still, slightly alter your meaning.

If your interview is to be recorded, you have every right to ask how much of it will be transmitted. Will it just be used as a news clip or will about four minutes of the tape be played?

When you arrive at the studio or while waiting on the telephone, you will be asked to give the studio some level. This means talking to them about anything so that they can judge how quietly or loudly you are going to speak.

Interview facts

An interview is a conversation with an aim. Astute politicians have become rather adventurous in recent years as they have tried to move the goalposts and turn an interview into a party political broadcast. Sir Robin Day, who has had wide experience of both television and radio interviewing, shows concern in his memoirs about the way in which some politicians have set a trend by failing to take part fully in an interview as a conversation (*Grand Inquisitor,* Weidenfeld & Nicholson, 1989).

Dr Peter Bull and Kate Mayer analysed eight interviews done during the 1987 general election campaign and they found that key politicians, including the former Prime Minister, Margaret Thatcher, and the then Leader of the Opposition, Neil Kinnock, evaded more than half the questions put to them. They avoided being interviewed by a variety of different methods including ignoring the question, acknowledging the question without giving an answer, questioning the question, attacking the question, attacking the interviewer, declining to answer, attacking opponents, repeating the previous answer, and claiming to have already answered the question just posed. In other words it is possible to agree to do an interview and then to ignore the interviewer and questions in such a way as to accomplish your personal objectives without answering a single question.

However, be aware of the effect on the listener when you are
being interviewed. Some of Margaret Thatcher's interviews were
masterpieces in evasion, but the positive effect on the listener is
questionable. The task of the interviewer and interviewee is to create an atmosphere of communication and conversation which will
give information to those who hear it. Listen to the questions and
answer them fairly.

Preparation for the interview

In the period between agreeing to take part in a radio interview
and actually arriving at the venue, make sure that you know in
your mind what you want to say. Write down two or three words
on a bit of paper; these headings will jog you into action. If you
cannot summarize what you want to say in this way you may well
have problems in getting your message across. Remember that
people only have a limited amount of concentration. Avoid documents, files, notes, and leaflets; if *you* cannot remember the points
you want to make, how will your audience retain them?

When you arrive, try to have a few minutes chatting with the
interviewer informally. You will rarely have longer than this if the
programme is live. If the interviewer is professional, he or she will
want to do this anyway. Sometimes, though, technical problems or
production errors mean that time might be limited.

The interviewer will probably try to relax you and outline the
areas that he or she thinks you ought to cover, probably giving you
the first question as a lead-in to the conversation. Ask them how
long you will have for the interview and bear that in mind. Do not
waffle too much at the beginning. Just before you go on air, smile,
take three deep breaths, and enjoy yourself.

Voice

The biggest difference between writing and broadcasting is that
the words are actually spoken and the way in which you deliver
your words is often as important as the words themselves. Do not
put on a "posh" voice for the radio — clergy can sound terribly
"religious" without meaning to. Laity sometimes resort to words
that they do not normally use because they are representing the
Church.

Remember that accents are back in fashion. These days a Scottish, Geordie, or Yorkshire accent is considered as good as a southern one by the BBC! Speak at your normal speed and avoid accelerating as the interview proceeds as a result of nerves. Try to avoid jargon. Use words that encourage the listener to really take in what is being said — remember that Christianity is littered with words that are not normally used in everyday life.

Use stories when you can. People like to hear place names and people they might know, particularly on local radio. An interview on housing needs and the desire of the local church to help will be much improved if you can refer to a homeless person by their first name or talk about the needs in your town. Keep the interview rooted in everyday experience.

Time

Keep a constant eye on the clock. Few interviews on the radio are longer than four minutes, which means that you have very little time to get your message across, but it should be adequate. Do not take too long in replying to the first question: be pithy and to the point. Try to end the interview on an optimistic and cheerful note.

OH, AND BY THE WAY...A FUNNY THING HAPPENED TO ME ON THE WAY HERE.

Sound words

You will be doing God and the Church an enormous service if you
manage to achieve a positive and fruitful effect as a result of a
radio contribution. All that I have said here can be applied to any
other radio performance. With scripted "Pause for Thought" contributions, remember to keep your voice upbeat and positive.
There are thousands of Christians of all denominations working in
the field of radio and bringing the gospel to Christians who are
unable to go to church as well as millions of people who rarely go
to church through choice. Any positive contribution we can make
through the medium of radio will be of great assistance to our
churches. Whatever your contribution, enjoy it!

TELEVISION TECHNIQUES

Television will not go away if we keep our eyes shut long enough. It is not a cock-eyed invention like the coal fired moon rocket or the left-handed spanner — destined to end up in a museum of industrial archaeology. Television is doing for human perception what the wheel did for feet. And like the invention of the wheel, its appearance marks a decisive turning point in human history. (C. Morris, *God in a Box,* Hodder & Stoughton, 1984, p. 9.)

Television has changed the nature of society in the twentieth century. We now understand world issues, places, and people in the light of the television screen, and the Church is not exempt from the influence of television. The way in which people perceive the Church is very often governed by the media, and because of television's extraordinary power the portrayal of Christianity via this medium has important consequences. The Church, though, can also use television to good effect, and is increasingly resorting to video-making and the small screen as an excellent form of Christian communication.

Ian Bradley suggests that "For most people today the most powerful source of religious influence is not the church down the road but the television set in the corner of the living room" (in *Marching to the Promised Land,* John Murray Publishers, 1992, p. 187). Not only is Bradley correct in saying that television itself has become a religion to many people; he also underlines the fact that many people encounter religious belief and ideas through the television set either in overtly religious programmes or in the news and current affairs output on local and national television

Bradley continues:

The fact that a quarter of the British population chooses to spend the early part of every Sunday evening watching what is essentially a church-based act of worship says much for the survival of a strong residual folk religion in our national culture. (p. 188)

His figures are correct, but the reasons that people watch programmes like *Songs of Praise* are far more profound than simply reasons of folk religion. Although church attendances have dropped over the past twenty years, religious belief in Britain remains an important aspect of many people's lives even if they do not regularly visit a place of worship. Therein lies a communication challenge for the churches in which television has a crucial role to play. Thora Hird, who for more than a decade has presented *Praise Be* on BBC 1, which has regularly attracted over 6 million viewers, has received thousands of letters from "non-churchgoing Christians". She recently told me during an interview with the Bishop of London that many people write to her and stress that it is through television that they are able to catch a glimpse of God and his Church.

Martin Field argues that "If Colin Morris is right and television is the only contact many have with the church, who can blame them if it is all they ever want?" (*Faith in the Media*, p. 112). Religious programmes on television have a particular style and reputation that many churchgoers actually find rather unappealing. Such programmes aim to please and entertain rather than demand commitment. They are a taster or an overture for a much more profound and meaningful religious experience. Countless times it has been said to me at funeral visits: "Oh no, she didn't go to church but she never missed an episode of *Songs of Praise*. She loved it." *Songs of Praise*, excellent though it is, is not in itself a passport to heaven. Indeed, many of the best religious programmes are either those that deal with a distinctly theological or moral issue or those that are religious in a secondary sense, but well rooted in the modern world and context. *Heart of the Matter* and *Everyman* are good examples of this.

Most local news magazine programmes on BBC and ITV contain religious film reports and debates about a variety of issues such as the role of women in the church, the new blues band in the local Roman Catholic Mass, the 100-year-old organist, or the church-school headteacher who is taking a party to visit the Archbishop of York. Many regions, after the main news of the evening on both BBC and ITV, regularly screen a religious story as part of their diet of local news and views. There are, therefore, overtly religious programmes and programmes in which religion plays a part.

This week alone, on the same day, I received requests for the Bishop of London to appear on two different programmes. One was Thora Hird's Sunday evening *Praise Be* mentioned earlier, and the other was a guest appearance on BBC 1's *Question Time*. Both requests are equally important, but both put religion in a very different context. Many would argue that *Question Time* is the greater challenge because the religious case needs arguing in a very secular context. Similarly, picking your favourite hymn as a guest on *Songs of Praise* is a lot easier than going on to your local news magazine programme to explain why you think your parish church is the latest to be vandalized after a spate of attacks in the region!

This chapter is to help you face up to the task of appearing on television, whatever the context. I do not want to say too much more about the theology of television because a great deal has already been written. However, we must highlight some very basic points.

TELEVISION TODAY

We are living in the middle of a television revolution. As well as the four established channels, the inexorable rise of satellite and cable television continues. The video transformation has already taken place and, by the end of the century, nearly 80 per cent of homes are expected to have a video recorder. The chances of local leaders in any walk of life appearing on television is increasing all

I'LL JUST GIVE YOU A TOUCH OF MAUVE EYE SHADOW TO
COMPLEMENT YOUR COSTUME, DEAR!

of the time. Christians need to be aware of what is involved in a professional approach to any form of television contribution.

People spend far more time watching television than listening to the radio. The UK average for television viewing is just over 24 hours per person each week. People aged 65 and over watch 50 per cent more television than the average. More than 40 per cent of people in the UK are watching television between 9 p.m. and 10 p.m. We know from experience how great a part television plays in entertaining, informing, educating, persuading and encouraging. It gives people a view of the world that they would not otherwise have and its role can be both welcomed and questioned. Both BBC and the ITV companies have a mixed diet of programmes, but retain a commitment to public service broadcasting. Religious, children's, youth, and minority programmes would be included here.

Frank Jefkins (in *Public Relations Techniques,* Butterworth Heinemann, 1988, pp. l94ff.) highlights the unique characteristics of television as a form of communication. This medium is usually watched in social rather than work settings; people generally sit down and are rendered immobile as a result of it, thus the people, places and things portrayed become more real as a result of sound, movement, and colour. Its disadvantages, though, are numerous. Jefkins points out how time-consuming it is and how little control one has over the final product as a contributor.

The wide range of programmes that a member of the Church might be asked to appear on is difficult to list, but some of the most usual ones that are popular are as follows:

- *News magazine:* a local television programme highlighting a local news story or feature.
- *Children's programme:* these frequently ask for contributions of a religious nature.
- *Religious programme:* a *Songs of Praise*-type programme where there is a religious understanding at the outset.
- *Debate style:* programmes like *Kilroy* are increasing in number on all television channels — both nationally and locally. They frequently tackle moral and religious issues.
- *Documentary programme:* because religion affects so many different aspects of life, you may be asked to make a contribution as a religious representative in an essentially secular programme.

Whatever type of programme you are asked to appear on, general principles will apply. Let's start, though, with the first contact from the television station.

WHAT SHOULD I DO?

In our discussion on radio participation we asked a similar question, but television also demands that other questions be asked too.

- Am I the right person to appear in order to represent the interest or cause?

- Will I look right on camera and be able to give a reasonable performance?

- What is the main point that I want to get across to the viewers?

- Am I sufficiently prepared and, if not, what should I do to make sure that I am by the time of the broadcast?

A STEP-BY-STEP GUIDE

Who's who

First we must establish who you will be dealing with in most television situations:

- *Researcher:* researchers are employed by nearly all television programmes to do basic background work on subject matter and people. They will often be the people who approach you initially. Whether you are the right person for the news or feature programme will probably be established as a result of this first contact.
- *Producer:* this is the person who is ultimately responsible for the content and direction of the programme. Sometimes the producer has assistants, but the researchers are also working on the producer's behalf.
- *Reporter:* if you are going to be interviewed, this will usually be done by a reporter who will more than likely be responsible for all the interviews in the programme.

- *Cameras:* if you are being filmed on location, you will meet the cameraperson carrying a mobile camera. If you are in a studio, there will probably be at least three cameras operated by a camera crew who will be looked after by the *floor manager.*
- *Sound recordist:* the person responsible for sound will stand in close proximity to the cameraperson at all times and will ask you to give voice level, etc.
- *Director:* the director is responsible for the overall feel and presentation of the material produced by the producer. You will usually only come into contact with the director in a studio situation.

Where and what?

An approach has probably come by telephone from the researcher of, let us say for convenience, your local independent television company's newsroom. They are doing a documentary for the 10.30 p.m. slot next Thursday evening about vandalism and one aspect of the programme is to look at escalating vandalism directed at churchyards and churches. They would like you to be the spokesperson.

The first question you always ask yourself is, "am I the right person for this task?" If you know someone who can do a superior job and who is better informed, do not let the attraction of a television performance cloud your judgement. At the same time, do not opt out because you feel threatened by the prospect of appearing on television. If you are the right person, approach the task with confidence!

Next you should establish what type of contribution the company would like from you. Is it to be a studio appearance, or a location shoot either at home or out of doors? Is it to be live or recorded? How much editing will they be doing and are they really looking for just a soundbite or a more considered debate ?

It is important to establish what line of questioning they are hoping to adopt and where the interview is to take place.

Studio interview

In many ways this is the easiest type of contribution once you have overcome the actual trauma of the set and all that goes with it. It is organized, predictable, and means that you do not have to worry about the problems that can be encountered on location. Below I offer one or two words of advice for when you are actually in the studio.

Outside location

If the producer of the programme wishes to film you at home or at work and requests an outside shot, it is important not to be nervous about people watching or to be distracted by passers-by. If the weather is inclement, make sure that you do not look too windswept, wet, or uncomfortable. If you have any say about the backdrop to the shot, think about it carefully. If the programme is about your church they will probably want the church in the background. However, if it is about striking catering staff at the church school it is not a good idea to have them chanting in the background with you trying to be reasonable on camera in front of them. Together with the film crew, attempt to find a location that is suitable for everyone concerned.

Inside location

It is often the norm for the researcher to ask if the crew can come and film you in your home or place of employment. It is worth while giving a bit of thought beforehand as to where the filming ought to take place. Usually the reporter or producer will have an eye to the kind of shot they are looking for and may ask you if you would mind moving a bit of furniture around to obtain the required shot. It is important that you compromise with them. Do not have a backdrop that you are unhappy with; at the same time, remember that they will want the best background shot possible in the circumstances. Once a crew start moving furniture, curtains, and pictures they do not always know when to stop, so again, compromise is needed.

Live

Wherever the filming is to take place it is essential that you establish whether the broadcast will be live or recorded. If we are talking about a location shoot it is unlikely to be live, apart from events such as local elections, *Children in Need* or the *Telethon*

when local television does more than its usual amount of live location reports. Studio interviews are likely to be recorded in advance
to allow editing. If the interview is to be live this is to your advantage in many ways, but it means that the pace and method of
approach will need to be more aware and the room for obvious
nerves is nil!

Recorded

You should always treat any broadcast as if it were live, even if it
is to be recorded. The problem of a recorded interview is as follows. Being aware that you can "do it again" often makes people
less meticulous; this can then lead to the need for editing and the
possibility of unintentional bias creeping in. This is not to suggest
anything unprofessional on the part of the crew; it simply means
that you have to be aware in advance of what may be done to your
contribution if it has to be cut.

Questions

You really do need to have an idea about the line of questioning
before the broadcast, and the interview should have a beginning, a
middle, and an end. If the questions are changed between you
agreeing to come into the studio and the time you go on air the
producer should let you know in advance. For the sake of simplicity, I am going to take as my main example a live, studio appearance, though much of what I underline as crucial also applies to
location shooting. I will add a few extra notes later, but let us now
come to the big day itself when you set off as a representative of
the Christian Church to your local television studio.

On the way to the studio

Make sure that you have a clear head. In the car, or on the bus or
train, remind yourself that you are going to be on television and
that you must contribute to the best of your ability. You should be
able to say in one sentence why you are about to make a contribution: "to put the Church's view" , "to counterbalance the argument
put forward", "to seek publicity" may all be possible reasons.

While you are pondering on the way to the studio it is important that you clearly formulate in your mind the *point* you are going to get across. You will not be able to read notes or crib cards on television as this would look awful. Make sure that you are fully aware of exactly what you want to say and let this settle clearly in your mind.

It is obvious by this time that you will have given some thought to your appearance! As with speaking to groups it is important that you look smart. If you are a clergy person it is usually a good idea to wear a clerical collar to identify yourself with the caption on the screen. A layperson should look sober, sensible and comfortable; outrageous or unconventional clothes could detract from what you are saying. Men should avoid sweaters at all costs unless it is an agreed part of the set. A conservative shirt and tie (for laymen) will make what you say stand out. Women should also look as smart as possible; it is advisable to avoid stripes and heavy patterns so that your appearance does not detract from what you are saying. Hair should be well groomed; in summary you should look smart and comfortable.

GET UP YOU FOOL, IT'S ONLY THE STUDIO LIGHTS
SHINING OFF HIS BALD HEAD!!

Waiting for access

When you arrive at the studio you will report to reception and then wait until the person assigned to looking after you appears. This can be a nervewracking time but it is important to try to relax. When you are introduced to the researcher or reporter you will probably be taken to an office or hospitality room where you will be given refreshments and a chance to talk. Always check at this stage your understanding of the agreement concerning the interview and contribution.

If it is a large television company you may well be taken to the make-up department. This is primarily to give you a bit of colour and to prevent a look of "shining" or perspiration on the screen. If you know that there is no make-up facility, it might not be a bad idea to get some powder and put it on your face yourself. This prevents you looking a terrible shade of white and stops perspiration shining through.

At the end of this, you should be ready for the interview itself. Take deep breaths and keep in mind what you are going to say.

In the studio

One of the most disconcerting things about going into a television studio for the first time is overcoming the array of lights, cameras, cable, people, and activity that are going on around you — as if oblivious of your presence. Judith Stamper, a well-known regional television journalist in the north-east who fronted many clergy training courses on television, always used to warn contributors of the need to "overcome the fear of everything around you as soon as you get in". Judith would say "Look around you. Know what is there and who is there. Then relax and forget all about it." In fact, this is not a point to be taken lightly. It is vital that you master your surroundings and that you are aware of all that is around you.

You will be put in a seat, a microphone will be clipped on to your clothes and you may be asked to tell the presenter what you had for breakfast in order for level to be sought. If the interview is live, this may have to be done in a very short amount of time indeed. You may be brought in during another presenter's piece or during a videofilm report. If it is not live it may not be quite so frantic, but studio space is crucial in local television and they may be rushed anyway. Remember the need to look composed, smile be pleasant, and enjoy the interview!

When the cameras roll

You will not be aware of anything different as far as the studio is concerned apart from the fact that everyone else is totally quiet during an interview. For a short time all eyes are on you! Do not look at the camera unless told to do so. Always look at the interviewer who should reassure you all the way through by a professional nodding of the head to urge you on. Do not cast anxious sideways looks at the camera to make sure it is still there! Always speak slowly and deliberately on television, and avoid cue cards and paperwork. You should have nothing in front of you at all unless you really can't remember that crucial figure or quote without an aid . You will find that the time goes much quicker than you imagine — four minutes in television time is like thirty seconds of normal time. In order to achieve a successful interview, Judith Stamper always insists that all you have to do (regardless of the questions) is:

1. Say what you are going to say (first question).
2. Say it (second question).
3. Say that you have said it (third question).

This reinforces the point you are trying to get across, may frustrate the interviewer a little (no bad thing) because you are sticking to your guns, and gives you an air of confidence and authority.

After the interview is over you may well be offered further hospitality and you will find that you will need to unwind a little because television (particularly of the live variety) is quite a tense affair.

Television is the media of the moment. It is changing daily and as it does so its influence on society gradually deepens and becomes even more powerful. Whatever contribution you are asked to make on television, it is worth serious consideration if only because the Church needs to be represented where people are.

HANDLING A CRISIS

Crisis Public Relations means planning to deal with the unpredictable. (F. Jenkins, *Public Relations Techniques,* Butterworth Heinemann, p. 295)

The Church is no stranger to controversy. Ever since the preaching of Jesus first made an impression on the community in which he was born, there has been a continuous and often difficult path of controversy to tread. The Church is frequently in the news because of what it believes and why, but doctrinal and theological controversy (in our own era, the debates on the virgin birth, homosexuality, and the role of women are good examples) is only one side of the kind of controversy that Christians face in a media-dominated society. These are what I would term "internal issues", when the Church is engaged in internal wrangling and debate.

By far the most difficult controversy or crisis to handle for the local church is an event or happening that attracts outside attention because it goes against people's expectations of the Church. Hardly a week goes by without a national story breaking that has some kind of loose connection with the Church. "Layreader spurned wife for teenage lover", "Schoolteacher in bizarre love triangle", "Vicar admits petty-vandalism charge", and "Nursery group to sue church council" are all run-of-the-mill tabloid page fillers. A Christian community that is seen to be vulnerable as a result of human sinfulness, weakness, and failing will obviously attract media attention. In the New Testament letters, there are frequent suggestions not only of theological wrangling and questioning but also of misbehaviour, jealousy, sexual impropriety and rivalry (Ephesians and Romans have numerous examples) In today's world these would, and still do, provide "good" news stories.

Journalists are trained to hunt out interesting stories, and there has been a lot of debate and discussion lately about the merits and standards of the media. It has to be remembered that a good story is a journalist's "bread and butter" and it is a sad fact of life that our churches provide the media with a significant number of stories, that they would rather not see in print.

Many such stories begin in the local community. Most reports to do with the Church that appear the *Sun* or the *Daily Mirror* will have come from a local news agency, newspaper, or radio station.

This is an example of the media feeding off themselves. So, for example, the churchwarden who is charged with embezzling church funds; the church school deputy head who admits to sexual liaisons with a pupil; the activity of satanists in the priory church-yard — such stories usually begin locally. They can then expand and mature into the regional and national press and, in so doing, become more and more sensational, blown-up, and highlighted.

Let me now give you an example of such a story which, I must stress, is entirely fictional, but contains various elements that fre-quently occur in such a situation.

The Reverend Peter Keith has been the Methodist minister at Trinity Methodist Church for four years where Mr John Smith has been the organist and choirmaster for more than eight years. Mr Keith is a lively, modern, almost charismatic, figure who has wide support in the church. Mr Smith, though, is not amused by his minister's modern tastes in music and the choir have found them-selves increasingly torn between the two men.

On Remembrance Day, an ecumenical service had been orga-nized at which Mr Smith and the choir were expected to play and sing. Ten minutes before the start of the service, Mr Keith realized that the organist and choir were missing. For the minister, this was the last straw and he wrote to Mr Smith informing him that his ser-vices were no longer required and sacked the whole choir in the process. The following scenario then emerges.

A typical sequence of events would be as follows:-

- The organist rings up the local newspaper and advises the reporter that he intends to go to an industrial tribunal.
- The local newspaper takes up the story and prints it on the front page. The minister makes a general comment which is then misquoted.
- BBC local radio rings up. The minister declines an interview, but talks off the record. Local television also rings and it receives the same response.
- The local independent radio station picks up the story. A reporter calls at the minister's house saying that he has inter-viewed two ladies at the church who have called his action "dis-gusting".
- A local news agency contacts the minister, saying that it is cov-ering the story for a national newspaper and would like a quote. The minister declines. The independent local radio quote is being carried in the copy, accusing the minister of "disgusting over-reaction".

- The *Daily Express* contacts the minister's house. One of the local councillors, who goes to the Roman Catholic church, has accused the minister of "petty mindedness and an unchristian attitude". This time the minister defends himself publicly. He makes a statement to the *Daily Express*.
- The *Methodist Recorder* contacts the minister. The minister feels that at last he has found an ally and explains exactly what happened. The *Methodist Recorder* decides not to print the story.
- The *News of the World* rings up. It has found out that the minister is a contributor to a "happy clappy" hymnbook and that he dislikes the traditional hymns advocated by the organist. The minister refuses to talk.

This "media feeding" has happened on many occasions in the past. As a diocesan communications officer I am frequently called on to assist or intervene at any of the above stages. There is a tendency for clergy to freeze when the media begin the process of investigation and probing. Laypeople, too, tend to regard such matters with similar concern and usually refer them to the clergy anyway.

So what can you do in a crisis situation? How do you handle a story you would rather not see in print? What is the best way of protecting the gospel while acknowledging the truth of a situation in a context where the media are hungry for news? In order to offer basic guidelines, using the example we have already outlined above, it is important to stress all that has already been stated in previous chapters, though here I will be particularly concerned with the newspaper journalists.

Some basic points need stressing at the outset:

- Remember that the Church ultimately represents Christian teaching and values. Anything falling short of that will probably be newsworthy.
- Understand the nature of the media and acknowledge that they have a job to do. Many journalists do not like covering stories that result in people's downfall but they are paid to do a job and must get on with it. We ourselves, remember, are often the first to read such stories.
- Remember too the need for a balance between internal and external details and information. Make sure that people within the church know what is going on as well. Do not use the media as a way of informing those whose support you might need. Tell them yourself.

Damage limitation

We return now to the Methodist minister who has sacked his organist and choir because they failed to turn out for the Remembrance Day service. The reaction of the organist obviously suggests that there is likely to be trouble but, for the moment, this is all you have to go on. The natural reaction is to hope and pray that things do not go any further, but it is worth considering how you would cope in the event of the media becoming involved.

First things first

- Make sure that people in positions of authority in your church know exactly what is going on. It is unwise to act in a politically sensitive area such as this without the support of stewards or churchwardens, church council members, other ministers or elders. It is useful to give them a very brief written statement marked "strictly confidential". You have then taken them into your trust.
- If a particular group is involved, it is essential that you communicate directly with them. If the Methodist minister had sacked the choir via the organist, he more than deserved the resulting hostility from the choir. The natural way forward is to convene a meeting to announce your action, and explain why you have decided to act in the way that you have.

    A statement such as the following would suffice:

    "Following the complete lack of support on Sunday at the Remembrance Day service, I have decided to dispense with the services of the organist and choir of Trinity Church. You are fully aware of the increasing difficulties we have had over recent months of which Remembrance Day was but one example.

    "Once a new organist has been appointed, all former choir members will be invited to reapply.

    "I would like to thank you all for the hard work you have put into the church music in recent years."

Such a statement highlights the thrust of the problem: *a breakdown in the relationship between the organist and minister.* Do not add to the thoughts you have put down on paper. If you believe that the decision is right, then you must stick by the consequences.

The telephone call

"Hello, is that the Reverend Peter Keith? I'm ringing you about alleged problems in your church in which it looks as if you'll have to give evidence to an industrial tribunal."

This could well be the moment you dread. The voice is that of the *Local Echo* and John Martinez, a reporter, is on the phone. You have several options:

- Say you have no idea what he is talking about and suggest he checks out his facts.
- Ask him where he got his information from and then tell him you will ring him back in ten minutes.
- Acknowledge what he says and go straight into conversation with him.
- Slam the phone down.

Of these, I suggest only the second or third are options you should consider. The second is definitely the most preferable unless you feel completely ready to deal with the matter. A reporter will usually want his information quickly, so it would be wrong to expect him to wait longer than ten minutes. Make sure you know the name of the reporter and newspaper and the telephone number.

We come now to the most crucial aspect of dealing with this kind of crisis. Before you even receive the first phone call, write down a brief statement of not more than three short paragraphs highlighting your response. If the phone call is completely unexpected, then jot down a statement before ringing back. You may well be able to obtain help from a local communications/press officer if your church has one. The statement should read something like this:

> "After serious thought and consideration I have decided to dispense with the services of Mr John Smith as organist following a breakdown in trust and understanding. The choir has also been disbanded.
>
> "The post will be advertised and a new choir enlisted as soon as possible.
>
> "I am very grateful to Mr. Smith for all that he has done to enhance the music and worship at St John's."

The statement does several things. It: *acknowledges* that there is a serious problem that has resulted in drastic action; *looks to the future* with confident authority and suggests that the decision was taken after careful thought; *is positive* about a subject (Mr Smith) which is the actual cause and "leaves a nice taste in the mouth"; *is succinct* and does not explain what does not need explaining.

Once the statement is written it is a good idea to type it out in double-spaced format and to keep it close to you as the process of feeding the information begins.

Ringing back

When you have prepared the above statement, (taking not longer than ten minutes) it is time to return the reporter's phone call. Only deal with the initial call immediately if you already have the statement prepared.

- Sound positive when you ring back. Do not be curt, short-tempered, angry, or upset. Make sure that you remember the reporter's name: this immediately creates a better rapport. The reporter has become a person whom you are accepting.
- Explain that you have a statement. Read it out to the reporter who will probably take it down in shorthand. To avoid error, you could offer to fax it if you have a fax machine available.
- Expect a series of supplementary questions. Generally speaking, it is a good thing to avoid these. Patiently explain that you have nothing to add and that you are sure you have provided sufficient material. Here, the reporter may become persistent. It is very important that you continue to be pleasant and stick to your guns. The less information you give, the more likely it is that the report will be accurate.
- Even though the media may now begin the feeding process mentioned earlier, you have had a strong input at the start. Be aware of the possible need to make supplementary statements if the story develops.

Finally, there are some more general points that we must note about handling the press in a "crisis" situation.

1. Always be prepared where possible. Think "media" and prepare responses and statements that will communicate your side of the events.

2. Don't panic if things seem to be going badly. The story may seem more serious to you (because you know

everything and the media doesn't) and it is easy for things to get out of context.

3. Newspaper reporters are not responsible for the final appearance of the story. It will be checked by a more senior reporter (not for its factual accuracy but for its relevance) before being passed over to a chief sub-editor who will put in cross headings, probably re-write the first paragraph, and add a headline.

    Headlines are aimed at grabbing the readers' attention, and to move them.

    Be realistic and don't blame the reporter for the final result!

4. Be aware of requests for photographs in a crisis situation. As mentioned in an earlier chapter, a photograph can only add to the drama. My advice, in the context of crisis and uncertainty, is to avoid photographs.

CRISIS? WHAT CRISIS?

5. Radio interviews will not be easy in that you will find it hard to read out the prepared statement as it can sound wooden, odd, and false. To do a radio interview you have to remember what you have said in the statement and then verbalize it in a confident and up-beat manner.

   Stick to your main point and keep on saying it, even if the interviewer tries desperately to sidetrack you or make you say more than you want.

6. Television is usually looking for the soundbite, as is radio, but a television programme will probably edit even more out than the radio journalist. So don't make statements that can be taken out of context. Take careful note of all that was said in the chapter on television techniques.

7. If the story is a difficult one that looks likely to run for a long time, it may be a good idea to issue several press releases as you go along. Also, remember that once the media know about a story it is usually to your advantage to be proactive in your dealings with them. Keep them informed; tell them what you can.

8. Ignorance of church affairs, theology, and denominational politics is widespread among the media. Don't expect them to know everything!

   Do not become too involved in your subject; keep it simple and go out of your way to explain things in a straightforward manner to the reporter you are dealing with.

9. If you make reference to other people in the process of conversation, it is absolutely essential that you inform them of this. Don't leave it to the reporter to tell someone that you have talked about them.

10. The most difficult question to answer I have left to the end. *How can you know if something is likely to grab a local or national headline?* The simple answer is you can't. It can depend on various factors including:

- The amount of news around on any one day. The most dangerous times are August and in late December when news is in short supply.

- The topicality of a particular issue.

- Local personalities who become involved in the dispute.

- The willingness of someone to "spill the beans" and distribute the information.

We can conclude, however, on the basis of wide experience, that the following categories of stories are "high risk", usually because they contradict the gospel that the Church stands for — at least, in the eyes of the media they do!

- Sexual misdemeanour always makes the headlines. Obvious high-risk categories here are sexual abuse of children, homosexuality, extra-marital affairs.
- Financial irregularity of any form is likely to make good copy.
- Extrovert clergy of any denomination doing something unconventional.
- Different faiths having different views or ecumenical rows.
- Sudden local tragedy which demands crisis-management skills, such as the Valley Parade fire disaster in Bradford in 1985.

I have had much experience of dealing with each of the above categories in the past and as a communications officer in London no one knows what each day is going to bring. The churches must be vulnerable, open to criticism, and subject to intense analysis because they are affected by human weakness and sin as are all human organizations. The truth is a precious commodity that the churches must face up to in the context of a mass media eager to hunt out that which makes news.

The ability of Christians to deal with the media in a crisis situation has not always been evident. There is a great deal that can be learned from a more professional approach.

A CHURCH AUDIT

We need to be less apologetic about what we believe and have a greater assurance in our faith. Our buildings need to be user-friendly so that people actually feel welcome when they come in." (The Bishop of London, Dr David Hope, Deanery Visitation, 1992.)

In the opening chapter I raised some basic questions about the local church and communication. In a media-saturated world it is important that we consider how we are projecting the Christian message in our own locality and community. Every aspect of a church's life and worship is important if we are to challenge people successfully concerning the good news that we are called on to share. So often, though, communication is at the *bottom* of our list of priorities and concerns. This chapter is a basic guide for all in the *local* church and it offers some essential advice on effective communication.

OUTSIDE

It never ceases to amaze me how some churches can look so uninviting and unattractive from the outside. The following items should all be looked at to check that you are giving positive signals to the world outside:

• Is there a notice-board giving the church's name, its denomination, and who to contact for further information?

Notice-boards are usually in prime sites in local communities and yet they can be outdated, scruffy, and lacking in imagination. People who regularly walk or drive past, or look out from the local bus, will see what the notice-board says and this is an important witness to the local community. Many churches also have a secondary board which carries an evangelistic message or challenge. These should be used sensitively (preferably avoiding the guilt approach) and should be changed regularly. If they are used to advertise church events and services, someone should be appointed to remove the relevant poster on the day of the event or the day after. There are many companies who can help with both notice-boards and posters. Remember, it is better to have nothing at all than something which is totally unrepresentative of what is happening inside. Use bright colours, attractive typefaces, and change notice-boards regularly.

- Is the porch or entrance to the church inviting? Do people feel that this is a place in which they will feel welcome?

When I arrive at a church for the first time I am frequently surprised at the lack of inventiveness and imagination shown by the congregation when it comes to the entrance to the building. People will feel more relaxed if the entrance is bright and welcoming. A few weeks ago I went into a church that had a bright "Welcome to St John's" notice in the porch. In my former parish at Embsay near Skipton we put up a board (with photographs of all the regular attenders) in the porch that said "Welcome to the family of St Mary's." This meant that people were greeted by faces rather than wood or stone. It was also a favourite venue for fresh flowers at weekends. At this point it might also be worth mentioning the need for a clear passageway for wheelchairs and other disabled people. In some churches the disabled find the physical struggle to get into church a communications hurdle they could well do without.

• Is the area outside the church clear of litter and are the garden and churchyard kept in good order?

This is one of the key problems faced by most churches because it usually means having young, fit, and willing people who will clear up litter, mow lawns, and keep weeds under control. It is very important, though, that the outside appearance of the church is taken seriously. There really is nothing worse than arriving for a wedding or a funeral and passing through a churchyard with litter everywhere and empty cans and take-away wrappers blowing in the wind. This is just as important for the outside impression given by the church, as a good and meaningful service is inside the building.

INSIDE

Similarly, what people actually see when they are seated *in* the church will have a great influence on them. Symbols, windows, banners, candles, flowers, and musical instruments are some of the most obvious things that people will look at when they are sitting in church. Once again, if we are going to make contact with people, there are some obvious questions to be asked:

• Can people actually hear what is being said?

An increasing number of churches have now resorted to using microphones where audibility is poor. These are expensive and do have their own problems (cost, servicing, quality, someone to be responsible for the system) but, generally speaking, they have improved on people's ability to hear what is going on in the church. In small chapels and churches this is unlikely to be a problem, anyway. All clergy should be capable of raising their voices to be heard if the building is of a reasonable size, but if people are actually telling you that they cannot hear, then something needs to be done.

A more crucial problem here is congregational participation in worship, particularly when children are involved. How many times have you been to a service where a reading, poem, song, or dramatic piece has been performed and you simply have not heard one word? Of course, the fact that the Sunday School are doing something is important in itself, but if you cannot hear what they are saying there is a crucial communications barrier.

Children and adults reading in church need to be taught to read clearly, slowly, and loudly. If they cannot be heard and microphones are not available, then the wisdom of putting on such productions in a formal act of worship should be questioned.

• Can people actually see what is going on?

I have sat in cathedrals and gazed at pillars of stone throughout two-hour services on more occasions than I wish to remember. In these instances, had it not been for the microphone I would have heard nothing at all. However, even in smaller churches it is not always possible to see what is going on and in a media-dominated world it is important that people can actually see something of what is taking place. Having a movable platform for special services is how some churches get round the problem, and an increasing number of churches have moved their altars forward so that they are closer to the people. Ironically, more ministers are using pulpits again because it makes them visible; standing on the same level as the congregation in a church seating 320 is not a good idea for those at the back. Seeing and hearing are two crucial aspects of worshipping the Lord.

• When were the heating and lighting last looked at for improvement?

Church architects and developers are more and more aware of the importance of good lighting and heating in churches. Sitting in a freezing cold church on a chilly November morning is not exactly a great incentive for getting people out of bed! Many people still use the excuse "It's so cold in there, I just don't enjoy it". We live in a world where central heating, air conditioning, and good lighting are taken for granted in public buildings and homes. For a church to be a welcoming place we need, despite the possible financial implications, to take a close look at whether or not we are communicating warmth, brightness, and a welcoming atmosphere when people come through the door. It may well be that for many years a church has existed on

poor heating, lighting, and visibility. Any church making positive plans and aiming at a successful evangelistic ministry must
ensure that the building is well lit and reasonably warm.

CORPORATE IDENTITY

Frank Jefkins makes a clear distinction between "corporate image"
and "corporate identity", suggesting that "a lot of nonsense is
talked about creating, improving, polishing and projecting a corporate image" (*Public Relations Techniques,* Butterworth
Heinemann, 1988, p. 268). He stresses that the corporate image is
mental and corporate identity is physical. He defines corporate
image as "the impression of an organization based on knowledge
and experience. Since everyone's knowledge and experience of an
organisation will be personal and will differ, the corporate image
will vary from one person to another" (p. 269).

It is therefore the cultivating of our corporate identity that is
crucial if people are to gain their own understanding of what we
stand for.

Most local churches are sadly lacking in internal coherence,
shared vision, and a common strategy. The choir has its own
agenda; the mothers' union feel that they are never consulted; the
people leading the youth groups rarely come to church; the leaders
of the uniformed organizations even less so. The men's fellowship
now meets outside the church building and the church council is
made up of people who live outside the area. Such a scenario is
very frequently found and the old adage that we must have our
own house in order before people will respond to us with commitment and understanding is very true. We need better internal communication channels in our churches; people need to feel as if they
count and belong.

If a successful corporate identity can be fostered in a church,
confusion and misunderstanding can be reduced.

A CHURCH LOGO

One of the most basic methods of establishing a feeling of a
church family across a whole range of groups and organizations
within the Church is by the development of a simple logo that is
used by all groups associated with a church. Jefkins reminds us of

the historical background here (in *Public Relations Techniques,*
Butterworth Heinemann, 1988, p. 272):

> *Centuries ago a king would lead his army and identify him-*
> *self by means of an emblem on his shield, such as the cross*
> *of St George or the cross of Lorraine. But since this was*
> *rather dangerous it became the fashion for all the king's*
> *knights to wear the same emblem, which was confusing to*
> *the enemy. Emblems became flags and later troops wore uni-*
> *forms.*

The development of livery, the use of logos, and the making up of
slogans all originate from the same historical background.
Christianity has, since the resurrection of Jesus, seen the cross as
its chief symbol and rallying point. It is the ultimate sign of the
Christian community in worship together.

More and more churches are now realizing that a well-drawn
and designed logo used across the whole of the church's life can
have a psychologically binding effect. Such logos can be used in a
variety of different ways and can incorporate various elements:

- the cross;
- a picture of the church;
- a well-known feature of the local community;
- a national coat of arms;
- a slogan.

Once a logo has been designed for the church it should be used on
everything associated with the church, including:

- all stationery;
- on the front of the church magazine;
- in all group leaflets and publications;
- on all posters;
- on the notice-boards outside the church;
- on all service leaflets/weekly noticesheets;
- in any local advertisments in the press;
- on any pens, mugs, tee-shirts, or tea towels sold by the church.

Many will question the communication of the good news of Jesus
in what might appear to be crass commercial terms. However, people do respond to something that seems to be communicating effi-
ciency, love, care, and unity, and many of the above items cost
little extra money.

A CHURCH DIARY

Another simple way of improving church communication is to establish a church diary in which all services, social events, meetings and special days are clearly highlighted. This would usually be kept with the church secretary though the minister may feel that this is something he/she ought to look after. Such a diary obviously means that clashes of dates and interests can be avoided and that people are kept informed in the weekly bulletin and parish magazine of all that is going on.

EFFICIENT MEMO SYSTEMS

It is dangerous to presume that people in church know what is going on. It is no good thinking they know— you have to make sure that information flows freely between church officers and members. Some churches have a simple memo system with the parish logo, etc., on the top and these are circulated to everyone concerned with the information being relayed.

A SPECIAL EFFORT

It may well be that your church is at a suitable stage to hold what we can call for our present purposes a "communications audit". At a meeting of the church committee it might be worth chewing over the following questions to see what areas of internal communication can be improved in your church.

- Is the exterior of the church up to scratch? Does it appear looked after, cared for, and attractive?

- What internal improvements can be made to enhance worship in the church (see below)?

- What improvements can be made to the church stationary?

- Have we devised an appropriate church logo ?

- When was the church magazine last reviewed and what improvements can be made there?

> • Are the church notices communicated efficiently and accurately?

LEADING WORSHIP

There has been plenty written about leading worship in the various Christian traditions and this is not an attempt to provide an exhaustive treatment of the dos and don'ts. Rather, we are here called on to consider some of the very basic communication points that enhance and improve any public act of person-to-person communication regardless of whether or not we are preaching, celebrating a sacrament, giving the notices, or leading a family service.

So often I visit churches and I am appalled by the lack of professionalism and commitment shown by clergy and laity in the leading and presentation of worship. Even in traditions where personality and individuality are not encouraged in worship, it is possible to be aware of some very basic points that enable the congregation to participate joyfully and discover even more depth and understanding in the service. Some of these will have been covered in earlier chapters and I merely summarize some of the key areas.

DO PEOPLE KNOW WHERE THEY ARE?

This is a basic question and yet it is obvious that many people go to church but have not got a clue about what is going on in the service. In a television age where everything is explained, such ignorance on the part of a congregation can lead to boredom, bewilderment, and a feeling of exclusion. At the same time, we don't want a series of announcements that interrupt the worship to the point where people feel as if they are back in the first form at school.

• Give an introduction at the start so that people know where they are, what the service is, what day it is in the life of the Church and, on special occasions (weddings, etc.), who *you* are. Unfortunately, we do not have a television facility to flash your name up on a big screen!
• Keep the notices together in one place. Do not keep interrupting the service with things you have forgotten to read out at the appropriate time.

- Check that hymn numbers are correct and that people can see them. If you are omitting verses, make sure that people know.
- Ensure that you are well turned out; that you look smart and clean, and that your appearance does not detract from the job you are doing.
- Organize the offertory before the service and make sure people know exactly what is involved.
- Always use microphones consistently. Do not switch from using them to abusing them!

Such matters are at the heart of a successful review of communications in any church situation. In many ways these things are just as important as how the church is perceived in and through the media because in a media-saturated society people's standards and expectations are so much higher.

We must seek to be more user-friendly and to show that we want to communicate the words and works of Jesus wherever we are. All local churches can improve their internal communication considerably and a regular review is to be encouraged.